MW00686195

THE WRITING DEAD

TELEVISION CONVERSATIONS SERIES
DAVID LAVERY, GENERAL EDITOR

THE WRITING DEAD

Talking Terror with TV's Top Horror Writers

Thomas Fahy

UNIVERSITY PRESS OF MISSISSIPPI / JACKSON

www.upress.state.ms.us

The University Press of Mississippi is a member of the Association of American
University Presses.

First printing 2015

∞

Library of Congress Cataloging-in-Publication Data

Fahy, Thomas Richard
  The writing dead : talking terror with TV's top horror writers / Thomas Fahy.
      pages cm. — (Television conversations series)
  Includes index.
  ISBN 978-1-62846-201-2 (cloth : alk. paper) — ISBN 978-1-62674-550-6 (ebook)
  1. Horror television programs—United States—Authorship. 2. Television horror
writers—United States—Interviews. I. Title.
  PN1992.8.H67F34 2015
  808.2'25—dc23   2014031612

British Library Cataloging-in-Publication Data available

"I JUST WRITE ABOUT WHAT SCARES ME. WHEN I WAS A KID, MY MOTHER USED TO SAY, 'THINK OF THE WORST THING THAT YOU CAN, AND IF YOU SAY IT OUT LOUD THEN IT WON'T COME TRUE.' AND THAT'S PROBABLY BEEN THE BASIS OF MY CAREER."

—STEPHEN KING

CONTENTS

Part III
ZOMBIES, MONSTERS, AND WEREWOLVES, OH MY

Part IV
"WHO YOU GONNA CALL?" HAUNTED HOUSES AND OTHER SUPERNATURAL TERRORS

ACKNOWLEDGMENTS

I want to thank all of these talented artists who generously took the time to speak with me about their work and about the diverse, dynamic, and devilishly fun genre of horror. Your creativity and dedication inspired this book, and I thank you for that as well.

I am also grateful for the support of Long Island University and the University Press of Mississippi. And finally, I couldn't have finished this project without the help of the usual suspects—my family, Tatyana Tsinberg, and Daniel Kurtzman.

INTRODUCTION

One can hardly turn on a television without coming across something horrifying—and I'm not just talking about Donald Trump's *The Apprentice*. Horror is everywhere on the small screen. Entire channels, like Chiller and to some extent Syfy, dedicate themselves almost exclusively to it. Dozens of cable networks rerun horror films on a weekly, if not daily, basis. Even the recent advertising campaign for the Independent Film Channel (IFC) features horrific images to entice fans. In one IFC ad, someone arranges vegetables on a cutting board. Moments before the knife is lowered, a row of carrots appears to be human fingers. Then a chopping sound can be heard before the network's slogan appears: "Always On. Slightly Off." (So much for tuning into the Food Network later!)

As these ads suggest, terror has become a hot commodity on TV. In fact, more horror shows are on air now than at any point in television history. *The Walking Dead*, which has the dubious distinction of having the highest body count on TV (with over 500 on-screen zombie deaths to date), is currently the most watched show on TV, and its October 2013 season premiere garnered over 16 million viewers. Its success has inspired a host of new dramas for horror fans that draw explicitly from iconic horror movies. *Bates Motel*, which was the most-watched debut in A&E history, offers a glimpse into the early life of its main character, Norman Bates. Likewise, the series *Hannibal*, based on characters from Thomas Harris's *Red Dragon*, depicts the early relationship between Hannibal Lecter and FBI profiler Will Graham. Veteran actress Jessica Lange won an Emmy in 2012 and 2014 for her performance on *American Horror Story*—a show that often feels like a montage of classic horror with its self-conscious allusions to everything from Mary Shelley's *Frankenstein* (1818) to Stanley Kubrick's *A Clockwork Orange* (1971). And as *True Blood*, *The Vampire Diaries*, and *Being Human* make clear, vampires continue to enjoy a thriving afterlife on TV.

So what explains the immense popularity of horror right now? In a genre that has traditionally appealed to young men between the ages of eighteen and twenty-five, what has finally convinced so many others—particularly women and older audiences—to watch? To see horror as something more than blood and guts? The answer seems to be the medium of TV itself. There is something about the nature of serialized drama that has increased the appeal of horror. Serial killers might be preying on a suburban neighborhood much like your own. Zombies might be trying to eat people. And vampires might be petitioning for the legal right to marry non-vampires. But in the safety of your own living room, these elements primarily function as a dynamic backdrop for watching characters develop, relationships unfold, and romances blossom. This depiction of intimacy is particularly important for the popularity of horror television. It not only intensifies our investment in these characters, but it also parallels the illusion of intimacy offered to fans through technology. Viewers have unprecedented access to TV actors, producers, and writers through websites, blogs, online forums for fan fiction, interactive video games, Twitter, and other forms of social media. This type of access to and opportunity for connecting with a show has built a vast community of viewers that actively responds to its favorite shows. Countless blogs recap each episode. Even *X-Files* fans are still signing online petitions for a third movie, twenty years after the premiere of the series! These outlets intensify personal investment because they encourage viewers to spend time engaging with a show far beyond weekly installments. As *True Blood* writer Alexander Woo recently explained to me, "the experience of watching television is analogous to a long-term relationship between friends. . . . The brain chemicals that are fired by watching episodic television are identical to the brain chemicals that are fired by having actual friends. It is emotionally the same experience! And anecdotally you know it to be true. The times when a show has really gotten under your skin you are happy for the characters when good things happen to them. You are angry with them if they do something that makes you mad. You fear for their welfare if they're in danger. And you talk about them with your actual friends the day afterwards as though they were real people." The Internet has certainly intensified such connections between viewers and characters, and this type of intimacy has helped make horror one of the most dynamic genres on television.

Horror TV is also popular because—let's face it—most of us like a good scare every once in a while. In Brett Martin's recent examination of the newest golden age of television, he attributes much of its quality to "narratively ruthless" writing: "It would no longer be safe to assume that everything on your favorite television show would turn out all right—or even that the worst wouldn't happen."[1] It almost goes without saying that no genre on television is more narratively ruthless than horror. These shows delight in creating dangerous worlds where the worst things happen all the time, and they do so, in part, because of the pleasure viewers get from taking these thrilling journeys. Stephen King once compared this aspect of horror and its appeal to riding a roller coaster. We enjoy the anticipation of terror, the mixture of fear and exhilaration as events unfold, the opportunity to confront the dangerous in a relatively safe context, and the feeling of relief when it's over. Whether this happens in an amusement park, a movie theater, or a living room, horror gives us the opportunity to realize, as King put it, that "the worst has been faced and it wasn't so bad after all."[2]

On one level, 9/11 created a new sense of terror at home, and horror TV has offered an outlet for these anxieties ever since—much as television shows like *Alfred Hitchcock Presents* and *The Twilight Zone* first tapped into Cold War fears of the 1950s. As part of this tradition, today's horror shows allow us to confront the apocalyptic in a context that enables us to overcome our fears. People endure in these shows, and in that way horror TV offers a comforting message. Likewise, during the moments when we recognize the behaviors of certain characters as monstrous, these shows affirm our humanity. They remind us of our own normalcy and sense of morality.

On another level, the popularity of horror television might also suggest that we are not seeking relief at all, that we are instead seeking to be shaken out of our own complacency. A growing disaffectedness among Americans toward the U.S. political system has raised profound doubts that the government can solve the country's most pressing problems—an anemic job market, ballooning personal debt, corporate corruption, and global warming. Yet consumer culture and the demands of daily life—from raising children to paying the bills on time—encourage most people to retreat into the comforts of television. It's easier to watch TV than camp out at Zuccotti Park, even when we recognize the need to participate in social action. The appeal of horror television might therefore come from a desire, whether conscious or unconscious, to be challenged, to disrupt the status quo. Horror television strives to make the viewer profoundly uncomfortable—not simply through cringe-inducing zombie makeup but through the choices that characters make—and in doing so it invites us to think about the choices we ought to make when our world seems out of balance or turned suddenly upside down.

The best shows on television (regardless of genre) come from the best writers, and there is no better way to understand this contemporary moment in TV than to talk with the people making today's most frightening and fascinating shows. In addition to revealing behind-the-scene glimpses into these shows, these writers discuss favorite characters and storylines. They talk about the things they find most frightening to write about. They offer insights into the writing process. They reflect on the horror works that influenced their careers. And they reveal their own personal fascination with the genre. The thirteen interviews in *The Writing Dead*, which I conducted from the summer of 2013 to early 2014, also reflect the changing landscape of horror TV—from the shows being produced by major networks and cable channels to shows made exclusively for online streaming services such as Netflix and Amazon Studios. Taken together, these conversations paint a picture of horror TV as compelling, sophisticated, and wickedly smart. From rabid fans to first-time viewers, from aspiring filmmakers and writers to anyone who wants to learn more about why we like being scared, *The Writing Dead* has a little something for everyone.

But just to be safe, you might want to read this book with the lights on.

TF

Notes

1. Brett Martin, *Difficult Men: Behind the Scenes of a Creative Revolution: From* The Sopranos *and* The Wire *to* Mad Men *and* Breaking Bad (New York: Penguin, 2013), 5–6.

2. Stephen King, *Danse Macabre* (New York: Everest House, 1981), 27.

Part I

BLAME IT ON MOM

Even Serial Killers
Need a Hug

Hannibal

AN INTERVIEW WITH BRYAN FULLER

Bryan Fuller may not be a culinary wiz when compared to Hannibal Lecter, but his newest show, *Hannibal*, is serving up some horrific dishes for horror fans. Fuller considers all of his work for television—as the creator and writer of the critically acclaimed shows *Dead Like Me*, *Wonderfalls*, and *Pushing Daisies*—to be inspired by horror. His television career started on *Star Trek: Deep Space Nine* and *Star Trek: Voyager*, and he also served as a writer and producer on the series *Heroes*.

Fahy: You seem to be having an awful lot of fun with food on *Hannibal*, so there is one question I'm dying to ask. Do you yourself cook and has Hannibal used any of your recipes?

Fuller: (laughs) I cook, but I usually use somebody else's recipes. The recipes that Hannibal uses are from Chef José Andrés who is a James Beard award-winning chef. He has been on *Top Chef*, has had his own show in Spain, and is a world-renowned culinary expert. I knew that Hannibal Lecter had to have a vastly superior culinary knowledge than I do, so I reached out to José Andrés. He was very enthusiastic about being the consultant on the show. He is a very interesting guy. Our first meeting happened when he had just won the James Beard Award, and I approached him at the reception: "Hi, I'm so-and-so, and I'm working on this Hannibal project." His eyes just lit up. He said, "You have to let me be the consultant for the food." And I told him, "That's actually why I'm talking to you because I want you to be."

He never got precious about the cannibalism. He always approached the dishes as meat is meat is meat. Therefore, if you're eating meat, you have to accept that human beings are meat, and that is a valid form of protein if there is no other one available.

There was an article that came out recently about what happened to the Missing Link between *Homo sapiens* and Neanderthals. What they determined was that *Homo sapiens* ate the Missing Link, which is why we can't find them.

Fahy: You are a long-time horror fan, and this show is not the first time you've worked with this horror in television and film. Had you been interested in working with the character of Hannibal Lecter for some time? And how did the show come about?

Fuller: Actually, it kind of fell into my lap in a very interesting way. I was on a plane ride sitting behind a friend of mine who had just become the CEO of Gaumont Television. She told me they had just acquired the rights to the Hannibal Lecter character, and she asked if I thought there was a show there.

My first response was, "Oh my God, I have to do this to make sure it is something I would want to watch." There are so many ways of telling a Hannibal Lecter story. I just wanted to make sure the version that we saw on the television show was one that I wanted to sit down in front of. So my motivation to work on the show was very selfish.

Fahy: Is there something particular about Lecter's character that made you want to get into his head, which, I would imagine, is a pretty scary place to spend time? Were you at all nervous about writing such an iconic villain?

Fuller: Well, it was actually scarier to get inside Will Graham's head because he is the one who is damaged by exploring these ideas. So you really have to get into the psychological head space of somebody who is not willing to be there. It's harmful to him to hunt these killers. Whereas Hannibal is kind of getting a kick out of what

Hannibal Lecter (Mads Mikkelsen) sits down to enjoy a good meal on *Hannibal* (NBC). "Aperitif" (Season 1, Episode 1). NBC/Photofest, © NBC.

he does. It is actually less traumatic to write for him in a way than for Will Graham. Lecter knows who he is. He has a confidence in his villainy that he is doing the right thing. My approach to writing him has always been to present him as the sanest person in the room. There is something very exciting about writing a villain who is so hyper-sane and protective of society and humanity in such an unorthodox fashion that he is willing to kill and eat people to protect the beauty of society as he sees it. There is a kind of fun quality to his attitude of eat the rude. (In the books, he refers to his victims as "free-range rudes.")

I really wasn't nervous about approaching Lecter's character in one sense because I had a clear idea of who he was and what chapter of his life was interesting to tell. My intention was to be very faithful to how he is portrayed in the literature, so I felt a confidence in my approach. As long as I stick close to the version that Thomas Harris wrote and did a lot of the heavy lifting in fleshing out, I'm going to be relatively safe. As a hardcore fan, I feel like I just have to

stay true to myself as an audience member because a) I'm very protective of the character, and b) very enthusiastic about the character.
So I'm kind of the right fan boy to do the job in an interesting way.

Fahy: Even with all of your experience, I would imagine that seeing
actors bring alive your writing must still be a thrill. Have there been
any performances by the actors in *Hannibal* that surprised you, that
made you develop a character differently than you had expected?
Fuller: All of them have been pretty surprising. I think Hugh Dancy has interpreted his character in such a delicate way that arguably
could be alienating in another actor's hands, but he has made it very
seductive in a fashion that the audience and myself feel protective of
Will Graham—because he is so unhappy, because he is such a sweet
puppy-soul of a man. (laughs)

We are horrified by the hoops that Hannibal has him jumping
through, but we are also rooting for his purity and humanity. As
Jack Crawford says, Will Graham is such a pure individual that he
will always come back to being himself. In a sense, Jack Crawford
has got a better understanding of Will Graham than Hannibal Lecter in that he understands Will as a pure being. Hannibal is betting
that Will Graham is not so pure if he can imagine these things, and
Will Graham is terrified of his imagination. In *Red Dragon*, Will
Graham views his imagination as a chair made of antlers, which
is grotesque but functional. I thought that was a really interesting
idea to run with. Will has a very centered self, but it is being thrown
into this calamitous storm of Hannibal Lecter's machinations. So
we worry if he is going to take on too much water and sink. That is
the journey of the first season.

The exciting thing about the second season is that Will Graham
hits rock bottom, and the thing that I'm very eager to write and to
see is how he comes out swinging. He is such a victim in the first
season, but in the second season, we are going to see a change in
how he deals with Hannibal Lecter. Will is going to be as sly and
manipulative as Hannibal was with him in the first season.

Fahy: Does that set the stage for moving the series more closely to the point where the story intersects with *Red Dragon*?

Fuller: Yes. I would argue that Will Graham was so psychologically traumatized by investigating the serial killer the "Minnesota Shrike" that he had to be institutionalized. I feel like we are well within the cannon of the literature, and it is about finding a way to come out of that darkness—to get Will Graham to a place in season four (our "Red Dragon" season) where he would be closely aligned with whom Will Graham was in the book. So I have two chapters to put Will through the ringer and to get him back.

Fahy: The show is particularly gruesome at times, which is certainly in line with the novels and the character of Hannibal Lecter. Is there a line you won't cross in this show?

Fuller: Well, I'm not interested in rape stories particularly. For me, most of the serial killers are about rape, murder, and control. As Will Graham says in the first episode, it's about a male penetrative control issue. The ripped from the headlines, true-crime nature of a lot of television procedurals doesn't have an appeal for me because I'm actually very, very sensitive—despite being such a huge horror movie fan. (laughs)

So I'm not a fan of horror movies where everybody dies. That is too nihilistic for me. But the horror we do on *Hannibal* is much more philosophical, psychological, artistic horror. Every one of our killers has some sort of philosophy behind their approach to murder that is honoring what Thomas Harris established with his villains. Take, for instance, the Red Dragon himself, a man in his mid-forties who is experiencing a midlife crisis of sorts and who feels a need to evolve into a super being that will be infinite. This desire is wrapped in certain childhood traumas. Or take Buffalo Bill who wants to be a woman so badly that he is making a woman suit out of real women. There is always this kind of kink to the murderers, and we really try to embrace that and reflect that as much as we can in the characters on the show. So we have a character like Elden Stammetz ("Amuse-Bouche"), who is a man looking for a connection because he understands the way mycelium reflects a lot of properties of the physical human being, yet this substance is better at connecting. That parallels Will Graham's feeling a pull to connect with Hannibal Lecter. Or we have Tobias Budge who is a serial killer who wants to recreate an authentic, dark sound that doesn't exist with modern musical instruments. He is literally taking his strings from human guts and teaching children how to play them so they have this larger-than-life, epic quality to them. That was also an interesting episode about whether or not serial killers can have friends ("Fromage"). We got to explore that in a way.

Every one of these killers has an interesting point of view on murder. For me, given my sensitivity, that approach places the serial killer above reality, so they are the work of fiction and art as opposed to something that is real that I don't want in my head. I don't want to think about horrible people who do terrible things to humanity just because they're assholes. And most of the time with serial killers that is the case. They are just assholes. What we are painting on the show are works of fiction. Hannibal Lecter himself is a work of fiction. As Thomas Harris says in *Red Dragon*, he is uncategorizable as a crazy person. He is not a psychopath because he experiences regret. He is not a sociopath because he experiences empathy. So what exactly is he? The most interesting answer I've heard so far comes from Mads Mikkelsen who says he is the Devil.

Fahy: Even though there is an artistic or aesthetic quality to the killers in *Hannibal*, I'm curious if your own work ever scares you when you see it come alive on screen? What is your reaction to seeing the finished product?

Fuller: It depends on when I see an episode. If I watch an episode right before going to sleep, it will give me nightmares. (laughs)

The episode where Will Graham is projecting the crime of Abel Gideon ("Entrée") in the institution where he viciously murdered the night nurse is so disturbing and violent. I loved Hugh Dancy's performance. When he comes out of that projection, he is on the verge of tears, rattled, and very emotional because it was such a terrible thing for him to imagine. After I watched it, I went to bed and had nightmares all night long.

Fahy: You've been talking about your passion for horror, but in many respects, the tone and subject matter of *Hannibal* is quite different from some of your previous shows, *Dead Like Me*, *Pushing Daisies*, and *Wonderfalls*. Has that been a difficult shift? Or do you see connections between these works?

Fuller: I absolutely see connections between them. I would argue that *Dead Like Me* and *Pushing Daisies* are horror stories, just told with levity and comedy and romance. Essentially, *Pushing Daisies* is a zombie story. All of the tension and thrills of horror are removed and replaced with romantic comedy, but a lot of the tropes are there with violent deaths and people coming back to life and horrible mutilations of the body. I see it as romantic comedy horror. And *Dead Like Me* is about a girl who becomes a Grim Reaper and starts taking lives as these creatures, Gravelings, are arranging horrific accidents for people who need to die at a given time to keep the balance of life. I see those as horror adjacent.

Wonderfalls is really about a woman who is losing her mind. Jaye from *Wonderfalls* has a lot of similarities with Will Graham in *Hannibal*. Will is a man who is losing his mind. We just told that loss of sanity with Jaye through comedy and romance to make it a little more palpable, but if you strip comedy and romance away, you would get a similar journey that Hugh Dancy's Will Graham is going through.

I feel like I put in a little horror in everything I do, but I just candy-coated it beyond immediate recognition in those early shows. Now with *Hannibal*, it is about the savory dessert as opposed to the sweet one. There are certain delicious, desserty qualities to the show for me creatively because I get to tell these wild, fantastic murders, but I ground them in a way that makes them a little more psychologically penetrative.

I feel like everything is of a piece, but definitely the tone of *Hannibal* is such a departure that I had to let go of a lot of my crutches like alliterative dialogue and long running sentences of characters' babbling exposition to make it more fun. But *Hannibal* is relatively dialogue light compared to anything else I've written because it has a sobriety to it.

Fahy: Every time I see Caroline Dhavernas's character, I think that there must be days where you're tempted to write one of those wonderfully sarcastic lines in the style of *Wonderfalls.*
Fuller: Absolutely. Every once in a while, those lines come in, and it is very tempting to write more of them. But I want to be true to Thomas Harris. I can't over dilute Thomas Harris with my own tone. I have to be very respectful of what the audience expects with a Hannibal Lecter story.

Fahy: I also wanted to ask you a few writerly questions. When did you first know you wanted to be a writer?
Fuller: It had occurred to me in film school that I had a knack for writing, but I realized then that it was way too much work. (laughs)

There was that aspect of being very cognizant of how much effort was going to go into making these scripts and writing them down. I knew I had a skill set for it, but I was terrified at embracing it because I recognized that it is a seething amount of work.

It wasn't until I was watching an episode of *Star Trek: Deep Space Nine* that I realized how they structured the show and told the story. A light bulb went off for me because the episode communicated a structure that was mathematical in a way. I could see the code of storytelling, and then I sat down to write my own *Deep Space Nine* spec script. I submitted it to the show, and I got invited in to pitch. I pitched a couple of stories, and then I got hired on *Star Trek: Voyager.*

Fahy: What were some of your early influences in horror?

Fuller: I loved the stalk and slash films of the late 1970s and early 1980s like *Halloween*, *Friday the 13th*, and *Black Christmas*. It was an interesting era of horror films that were disregarded at the time as "B" movies, but if you look at them now and compare them with some of the remakes of those films, you recognize what was so great about the originals. You can see a disconnect from the writers and producers of those remakes with what made the originals so great. To take an example, *Friday the 13th* was about a bunch of really good kids who were doing their summer work to help children, and you care about these kids when they die. But the remakes feature one asshole after another. They're either masturbating in public places, or they're weed-obsessed or sex-obsessed. So the remakes feel like they are the remakes of the really bad sequels as opposed to the originals, which had an emotional core and a story that was relatable in some sense.

My two favorite horror films are *The Shining* and *Rosemary's Baby*. *The Shining* is deeply psychological, and it's also about a writer losing his mind, which I can relate to. *Rosemary's Baby* is a much more subtle version of horror but no less effective because it is an exercise in paranoia: *Do I know my partner? Do I know my neighbors? Can I trust my doctor?* Those types of horror films are very grounded in a sense, but then they kick things up a notch with moments like: "Oh, you're actually carrying the spawn of the Devil!"

Fahy: So as a writer in this genre, you are confronted with fans that crave both novelty and the familiar. How do you keep it fresh as a writer?

Fuller: For me it is all about the character and their story as well as the tone. There is always going to be a killer of some kind, so to keep it fresh you want to ask, a) what is that killer's approach?, and b) how does that killer's approach affect your protagonists—by either damaging them or getting under their skin in some way?

In a sense, I think *Hannibal* has elements that are fresh, but it has many more elements that are tried and true and well explored not only in the Thomas Harris literature but in all the movies that have been adapted or been inspired by that literature. Harris's books are really a brilliant hybridization of the crime thriller and the horror story. That is often what it takes to freshen up an old standard—to do a mash up with another element of a different horror story so that the blend is what is fresh and new in terms of tone and story. At the same time, your character always has to be somebody who has a distinct point of view on the event, otherwise it's another last girl desperate to survive the night.

"THE BLOOD OF A GOOD HORROR MOVIE IS A CHARACTER YOU REALLY RESPOND TO."

—BRYAN FULLER

Fahy: Would you say that is one of the biggest pitfalls of horror writing—when characters take a backseat to a good scare?
Fuller: Absolutely. I think it's a lack of understanding on the part of a producer or writer or storyteller to think that character isn't as pivotal as the other details in the film. It absolutely is. Take *The Descent* as an example, which I think is one of the best horror movies in the last ten years. It is filled with wonderful characters that are deeply likable, fresh, and appealing. Then you throw them in a cave with monsters, and they all react to the best of their gifts as human beings. You root for every one of them. There is not a single death in *The Descent* that doesn't hurt the audience because all of those actresses are intensely likable and effective in bringing those characters to life. The blood of a good horror movie is a character you really respond to.

Look at the original *Halloween*. You have Laurie Strode, who is immensely likable, and you have her fresh-faced American friends

Laurie Strode (Jamie Lee Curtis) reacts to some of Michael Myers's handiwork in *Halloween* (1978). Directed by John Carpenter. Photographer: Kim Gottlieb. © Compass International Pictures.

Annie and Lynda, who are incredibly likable as well. When they die, it's terrible! It's terrible when Annie gets into that car and notices the fog on the window. You are rooting for that character. She is real, honest, and accessible. Then you look at the remake of it, and they're all just assholes. (laughs) They are sort of trashy, unlikable, and vulgar. There is a lack of humanity in them, so their deaths are meaningless because we don't care. I didn't care.

I was actually so heartbroken because I thought Nancy Loomis, P. J. Soles, and Jamie Lee Curtis crafted amazing, accessible characters that were a joy to watch when they were alive. So when danger struck, it was terrifying for the audience because we genuinely cared about them. I cared about Adrienne King in *Friday the 13th* and Amy Steel in *Friday the 13th Part II.* I cared about them because the actresses were elevating their characters, so I felt like I knew them. They felt real. Their characters weren't hinging on a bunch of hacky tropes like kids using marijuana, which just takes the genre down.

In the same way, I thought Eli Roth's *Hostel* was very successful because those guys (the two lead protagonists) are very likable. They are in this terrible situation in which we see them die horribly. But Roth crafted an interesting, hyper-violent interpretation of the modern horror movie that still gave you character worth. The same happens with Sigourney Weaver in *Aliens.* She is a scrappy outsider that everybody resents for having a play-by-the-rules personality, but ultimately she is the one we are biting our nails for because we got to know her. We got to see her as a human being before the egg hatch.

Fahy: To continue with your thoughts on writing, what is the best criticism you've ever received as a writer?

Fuller: It's usually has to do with making it more emotional, more honest. "More character" is a note that I love to get. The notes that I hate to get are exposition notes. Those drive me crazy. The exposition is important, but if you don't have a character waving that flag, it's going to be on the ground and no one is going to feel moved.

Fahy: Is that one of the reasons you chose to adapt Stephen King's *Carrie* as opposed to one of his other works? Was it her character that inspired you?

Fuller: Absolutely. The character of Carrie is wonderful—so well thought-out and complicated. She is also human, in a way, where she can get ugly when she is pushed. In the version we did, we played her more as a victim who goes into a trance and kills every-body on a whoopsie accident, which was sort of a cop-out. That was to set the story up for a series because the network wanted it to be a TV series that followed Carrie after she survived prom night. How could the audience root for her if she willingly killed everybody at the prom and ran rampant through the town? The honest ending is that she has to die, which is why it's so effective in the literature. I'm very curious about Kimberly Peirce's new film of *Carrie* with Chloë Moretz and Julianne Moore, which is a fantastic bit of casting. I'm really eager to see that story.

Most of Stephen King's stories are character driven. I'm a big fan of *Pet Sematary*, and I would love to get my mitts on that. That story is all about death, the loss of family, the nature of family, and the man's role within the family unit—how far must he go to protect and preserve his family? It is such an interesting tale set against the backdrop of the Micmac Burial Ground, that awful cat, and dead baby Gage. There are so many wonderful elements to that story. Though I feel like the film adaptation was a fun horror movie, it didn't quite get all of the elements at play. I'm not afraid of remakes as long as there is something that has the capacity to grow in some way. A remake is valid if it is growing and evolving in ways that make it more true to the source material.

I also feel there is a valid remake in *Christine*. When John Car-penter brought it to Southern California, I felt that the story lost the impact of the cinema of the literature. The icy, snowy Maine landscape and that blood-red car against the backdrop of vast fields of snow were so poetic in the book. When you put it in sunny Southern California, you take half of that icy evil away and replace it with something else entirely. To be fair, I love John Carpenter's film. I think it's very effective.

As somebody who is a big reader and fan of the literature, there are always things that I notice or nuggets that I feel somebody missed. That is very much how I felt about *Red Dragon*. There is this great nugget of Will Graham that I had never seen explored in the literature, so I was really excited about digging into Will Graham in terms of my interpretation of the character based on the book.

Fahy: We've been talking a lot about film, but your own career has mostly focused on television. Were there certain TV shows that made you feel that TV was the right direction for you as a writer?
Fuller: Certain shows were very influential for me—*Twilight Zone*, *Star Trek*, *Twin Peaks*, *The X-Files*. These shows pulled you into the characters and the mythology so powerfully. What I recognized was that television gave the storyteller the ability to continue telling the character story after fade to black and to keep that character growing and evolving. That is very seductive to me as a writer. You tell smaller stories for characters in film. But in television, you get to explore so much more than you would get to in 90 to 120 minutes.

Fahy: The opportunity to have an extended relationship with characters does seem to be one of the really exciting things about great television.
Fuller: I completely agree. I think there is some great horror television on right now. I love *American Horror Story* and *The Walking Dead*. There are some great examples of wonderful horror story telling on TV.

Bates Motel and *Lost*

AN INTERVIEW WITH CARLTON CUSE

Carlton Cuse's early years in Hollywood were far from glamorous. As a personal assistant to a film producer, he often found himself doing odd jobs like buying organic dog food and getting the windows tinted on a car. After working as an assistant producer on the film *Sweet Dreams* (1985), he began his writing career in television on the Michael Mann series *Crime Story*. From there, Cuse went on to create and produce several shows, including *The Adventures of Brisco County, Jr.*, *Nash Bridges*, *Martial Law*, and *Bates Motel*. Before turning his attention to the life of Norman Bates, he spent six years as the show-runner and executive producer of *Lost*.

Fahy: I wanted to begin by asking you a bit about the wonderful set for the show. The iconic Bates house seems to loom over everything that happens. It almost acts like a character. Do you ever find the cast and crew getting caught up in the creepy mood created by that house and the motel?

Cuse: I would hope so. Part of the reason to do a show like this is to connect our story to the legacy of the original movie. Our production designer, Mark Freeborn, actually got the original plans from Universal that Hitchcock used for the constructions of the motel, the staircase, and the house. That was an exciting part of the process, to go back to the archives to develop the set. As writers, our goal was to bring Norman Bates to life. My writing partner, Kerry Ehrin, and I set out to redefine Norma and Norman's relationship. In the film we don't get to know Norma. She is already dead. So we wanted to create a whole new story—something that would be

Norman Bates (Anthony Perkins) beside the Bates House from Alfred Hitchcock's *Psycho* (1960). The set for *Bates Motel* was modeled specifically on Hitchcock's original. Paramount Pictures/Photofest, © Paramount Pictures.

different from the expectations of the audience. We didn't want to be bound by or beholden to the original. We wanted to create something new that would energize us as storytellers.

Fahy: Was it at all intimidating to take on such a classic horror film like *Psycho*?

Cuse: I wouldn't say intimidating. I would say challenging. Sure, there was a lot of room for failure, but we saw it as an enormous opportunity. Of course, we were really interested in the idea of how Norman Bates became the guy in that movie. It's a tragic story. But we also wanted to explore the loving relationship between a mother and son. There is a beautiful story to tell in that relationship. We wanted the audience to fall in love with these characters, particularly Norma and Norman. As their relationship unfolds, there is always that underlying tension that comes from knowing their fate, and for us that offered exciting possibilities as storytellers.

Fahy: What first gave you the idea to explore Norman Bates's early life as a television series?

Cuse: I was approached by Universal Television and A&E. A&E had already decided to do a series based on the *Psycho* franchise. They felt there was a good audience for it. The more I thought about the idea the more engaged I got with it. I also found the network really open to my ideas for the show. I had the idea of doing a contemporary prequel. By setting the story in the present, I thought we wouldn't feel as if we were walking in the long shadow of the movie. That way we could take this iconic material and spin it out to tell a new story. I also came up with the idea of giving Norman a brother. I thought it would be really interesting if Norman had a brother who was more of a "normal" guy. Then we could explore the dynamic of a mother with two sons, and the son whom she loves more, whom she considers to be "good," is actually the one in the most trouble. I felt that had some interesting possibilities.

It was Universal that brought Kerry and I together. She had already signed a deal with them, and they suggested we meet. So I sat down with Kerry, and we immediately hit it off. She had her own subset of ideas, which were wonderful. She was particularly interested in exploring the nuances of the characters and their relationships with one another. Once we started sharing ideas, we realized that our two subsets of ideas fit together quite well. It was a fantastic creative collaboration, and it has taken the show in compelling, unexpected directions.

Fahy: Had you always been a fan of Hitchcock's work?

Cuse: Very much so. So many of his films—*Psycho, Vertigo, Rope, Rear Window*, and I'd say *North by Northwest*—have had a tremendous influence on me as a filmmaker. Hitchcock had the ability to combine a humanist story with suspense. He could also sustain those moments of suspense and make them feel real. So in certain ways, I think the character-based thriller owes a great deal to Hitchcock. Certainly, there are elements of the show that are Hitchcock-inspired. The broad movement of the show parallels the original *Psycho* in that there is a murder, a cover up, and people investigating a crime. Those elements exist in the original as well as our own. But beyond those moments, we approached this series with the idea of telling the story of these flawed and tragic characters in our own way.

I think Stephen King has the same gifts [as Hitchcock] as a storyteller, and I greatly admire his work as well. Both Hitchcock and King have created these iconic works that take hold of you. Like a great painting, their works maintain a vitality and freshness. It's what I hope to achieve in my own work.

Fahy: One interesting aspect of Norman's character is that he doesn't remember his own acts of violence. He doesn't remember killing his father, killing his English teacher, assaulting his brother. I wonder if you could talk a little bit about that aspect of Norman. Why did you want him to have these blackout moments?
Cuse: In part the blackouts are connected with his dissociative identity disorder. People who suffer from that illness often have no memory of their actions. Part of Norman's journey is one of self-discovery. I guess one could say that about most characters, but in our case, it is particularly true. Norman is struggling to figure out who he will become. We know where he will end up because of the film, but the journey needs to be a surprise as it unfolds.

Fahy: So is *Bates Motel* a show about the missed opportunities that could have changed things for Norman, or is he fated to be the killer that we eventually see in *Psycho*?
Cuse: It's true that he is fated to some extent, but we still want the unexpected. We still want to surprise audiences with the stories we are telling. Yes, there is a dark inevitability to Norman's story, but if that outcome is too clear, the story will feel predictable. Good horror needs to surprise the audience. How Norman gets to that

place is filled with exciting, tragic, and horrific possibilities. Those possibilities interest me as a storyteller.

"GOOD HORROR NEEDS TO SURPRISE THE AUDIENCE."

—CARLTON CUSE

Fahy: You also decided to make the town a strange place—a place with a dark and dangerous underbelly. Is this a reflection of Norman in some way or another example of the way he is doomed (by his environment, his family) to be a killer?

Cuse: We really liked the idea of having the town be a metaphor for the dark and dangerous qualities of human nature. It becomes an image for the way the actions of the characters have consequences. Norma moves to this bucolic town thinking that she will be able to build a better future and provide for herself and her son. But the place—like the people in it—has this dark underbelly. Its secrets—like the thriving drug trade—offer great storytelling possibilities.

Fahy: Even with all of your experience as a television writer, I would imagine that seeing actors bring alive your writing must still be a thrill. Have there been any performances that have surprised you, that have made you develop a character in a certain way?

Cuse: Vera Farmiga brought so much talent to the role. Kerry and I wanted Vera for the show from the beginning. She was our first choice, but you don't always get your first choice in television—especially when you're looking for someone as accomplished and successful as Vera. She had gotten an Academy Award nomination for *Up in the Air*, so we didn't think she'd do a television series. But she really responded to the character. Sometimes as a writer, you are placed in the situation where you write a role based on the limitations of the actor. Not everyone can do what you want, but with

Vera, she can do anything. There is nothing we can write that she can't do beautifully. It's amazing to work with someone who takes what you have written and makes it better. And I would certainly say the same about Freddie Highmore as well. I defy you to find a better cast for these characters than we have. We're incredibly lucky.

Fahy: Do you feel that your work on *Lost* shaped your approach to *Bates Motel*?
Cuse: Of course. It's impossible not to be. One element that I brought to the table from *Lost* involved twists and turns. We always tried to surprise the audience on *Lost* with twists and turns. Sometimes those surprises thrilled or shocked the audience. Sometimes those twists upset them. So my experience writing those types of suspense stories—like my experience writing cop shows—has stayed with me. Likewise, Kerry brought her experiences writing nuanced characters from *Friday Night Lights*. We each had our personal experiences as writers that we brought to *Bates Motel*.

Fahy: In some ways, the series *Bates Motel* reminds me of the backstory sequences on *Lost*. If we were watching *Psycho*, I could easily imagine cutting away to an episode of *Bates Motel* to learn about Norman's introduction to taxidermy, for instance. Both shows used the backstory as a rich way to develop characters.
Cuse: I think that is fair to say.

Fahy: When you look back at your work on *Lost*, do you have a favorite episode or an element about the mythology that you are particularly proud of?
Cuse: It was incredible to be part of a show that tapped into the popular zeitgeist for such a long time. As a writer, your job is not complete until you have an audience responding to your work. To have such a big audience that was so invested in the show and the characters was amazing. You can go your entire career without having a moment like that. So we knew it was something special at the

time. The audience cared so deeply about what happened week after week—all the peaks and valleys. The show was also happening at a time when social media was evolving on the Internet, so what we were doing on *Lost* was being discussed by audiences all around the world. There was such an immediacy to what we were doing. Fans were responding to all of the choices that we made—whether it was about the guy in the hatch, Charlie's death (which upset a lot of people), or the first flash forward.

Ultimately, our goal was to tell good stories and to create characters that people cared about.

Fahy: I'd like to shift the focus to more writerly questions. When did you know you first wanted to be a writer?

Cuse: I had always loved reading, but in the fifth grade when my teacher started reading [C. S. Lewis's] *The Chronicles of Narnia* to class, I was completely taken in. I made my mom buy the books because I couldn't wait to hear the next chapter. I realized that I was not only connected to the art of storytelling but to episodic storytelling. That was the first time I realized someone actually wrote that, someone did that. From that point on, I knew I would write. I've always been interested in the way people are pulled in certain directions. Once you realize that you're good at something, it has a way of pulling you toward it. We all end up drawn to things. Just as musicians and artists are drawn to their crafts, I had a deep pull to be a writer. I knew I was going to writer whether or not I could earn a living at it. Ever since, writing has been a way for me to work out the issues of my life. It has been both a means for expression and for the therapeutic.

When I went to college at Harvard, I met the producers of the film *Airplane!*, and I arranged a screening of the film on campus. It was the first time I had met someone who made movies, and a light bulb went off. That experience started me on a path to being a filmmaker. I moved to Los Angeles and started working as an assistant for a producer, which meant I bought his organic dog food and got his windows tinted. It was a long road, but I kept writing. I got to the point where I had honed my craft and got good enough to get my work taken seriously.

Fahy: You've mentioned some of your early influences like Stephen King. Now that you are writing in the horror genre, what are some of the challenges? And how do you strike a balance between the familiar conventions that fans crave and their desire for novelty?

Cuse: I think ultimately it is about good storytelling and good characters. Yes, fans are interested in the familiar, but they don't want to hear the same story again and again. They want something new. What makes horror such an exciting genre is the way suspense and terror unites to thrill an audience. Audiences may want to take a familiar emotional roller coaster ride, but they want it done in a new way. I've been pigeonholed in different ways throughout my career. For a while, I was pigeonholed as someone who wrote cop shows, and after I did a couple of martial arts shows, I was pigeonholed that way. Certainly, no one expected a guy who created *Nash Bridges* to do *Lost*. No one expected Damon Lindelof, who had done *Nash Bridges* and *Crossing Jordan* (another police procedural show), to do *Lost*, but we steered at the helm of that show for six years. In some ways, I think it is an advantage that I haven't done much horror before. I love the genre, but my interest is in the stories and the characters. I hope that focus will keep the show exciting and fresh for audiences.

That is another thing that makes Stephen King so great—as great as any novelist in my opinion. He creates characters that are believable and puts them in the darkest places imaginable. He knows how to confront real, believable characters with the horrific in ways that engage and move his audience. If I can accomplish even a fraction of what he does, I would be happy.

Fahy: What do you think are some of the biggest pitfalls of horror writing?

Cuse: When the plot becomes more important than the characters. If the plot primarily drives the narrative (moving from plot point a to plot point b to plot point c), it doesn't give the characters time to get there psychologically and emotionally. So we become detached from the characters. Horror is not good when it feels mechanical and when we feel detached from the characters. You always need to combine a believable human story with that real sense of danger.

"WHAT MAKES HORROR SUCH AN EXCITING GENRE IS THE WAY SUSPENSE AND TERROR UNITES TO THRILL AN AUDIENCE."

—CARLTON CUSE

Fahy: What is the best criticism that you ever received as a writer?
Cuse: This goes along with something I said before. The best advice I received was to follow the characters, to view the characters as more important than plotting. I learned that from Bob [Robert] Getchell who did *Alice Doesn't Live Here Anymore* and *Sweet Dreams*, which was the first film I worked on. It is a simple idea but a wise one—one that has been incredibly valuable to me.

Dexter

Scott Buck began his writing career in Hollywood on the sitcom *Charlie Hoover*, and he continued to work on sitcoms for several years, penning episodes for a variety of shows, including *Everybody Loves Raymond* and *Coach*. In 2002 he joined the writing staff of *Six Feet Under*, and his work on that show paved the way for *Dexter*. Buck joined the writing staff of *Dexter* in 2007 and became the showrunner for its final three seasons. Before *Dexter*, Buck had not spent much time with the horror genre, so how does he feel about it now? As he told me during our interview, "I've seen enough dead bodies for a while—at least for now."

Fahy: When did you first know that you wanted to be a writer and what was the path that brought you to TV writing specifically?

Buck: I actually knew I wanted to be a writer at a very young age—by thirteen. In junior high school, I was already writing short stories and knew that writing was eventually what I wanted to do. I went to UCLA and majored in English. At that point, I was thinking that I wanted to write short stories and novels, but really as soon as I got out of college, I started writing material for television and screenplays. My father was a reporter for the Associated Press, and he covered television. So TV was always something I was aware of—not just because I watched it but because I was aware of it through his work. So I spent my entire twenties writing script after script after script and getting nowhere. I finally landed a job as a production assistant for David Milch. That soon led to me getting an agent and getting my first writing job, which was on a very early Fox sitcom called *Charlie Hoover*, which starred Sam Kinison and

Tim Matheson. I worked sitcoms for quite a few years until I made the move to *Six Feet Under*, which was my first hour-long drama. It wasn't necessarily a conscious choice from comedy to drama. It was just the fact that *Six Feet Under* was the best show out there that offered me a job. It turned out to be a very good move on my part to work on such an excellent show. But it was not necessarily a calculated thought at the time.

In one sense, making that shift taught me how to write in an hour-long format. *Six Feet Under* and *Dexter* are both also character-based shows, but that is something that didn't just come from *Six Feet Under* but every show I worked on—I mean, sitcoms are all very character-based as well. But learning how to tell a story that will last from the beginning of the season to the end of the season is not necessarily something you do in a half-hour show. It's learning to thread a story throughout twelve episodes.

Fahy: It seems like a fairly big shift from some of those shows to your work on *Dexter* in terms of subject matter. Prior to *Dexter*, did you ever imagine that you would spend so much time thinking about serial killers?
Buck: Never in a million years. No. It never sounded like the area I would sort of work in. What drew me to the show was that it wasn't just about serial killers; it was about this really interesting lead character named Dexter Morgan who was very complex—not quite this, not quite that. So it gave a lot of room for developing this person and finding out who he is and why he does what he does. This show also had a dark, very subversive sense of humor.

But horror in general was not a world I was very familiar with. There were a number of other writers on the show who were very familiar with the horror genre and were able to constantly reference it. But it was all new territory for me. Working on *Dexter* has made me intrigued by the horror genre, but I would also say for the time being that I've seen enough dead bodies for a while. (laughs)

At least for now.

Fahy: Horror has typically appealed to young male audiences. In terms of demographics, who has *Dexter* appealed to the most and why?

Buck: We actually have a pretty broad audience, and it appeals very largely to women. We have a huge female audience component. Again, I think that is because of the central character himself. This is a killer we kind of feel for and care about. We can see that he doesn't necessarily want to do the things he does, but he feels compelled. In some way, I think everyone can sort of identify with that—certainly not that we want to kill people but that we don't always do what is in our best interest, that we don't always do what is right, and that we often feel compelled to do things that we probably shouldn't do.

I think that aspect of Dexter's character appeals to men as well, but a richly developed, complex character with a really full emotional life seems to bring a female audience into a show.

"I THINK EVERYONE CAN SORT OF IDENTIFY WITH [DEXTER]—CERTAINLY NOT THAT WE WANT TO KILL PEOPLE BUT THAT WE DON'T ALWAYS DO WHAT IS IN OUR BEST INTEREST, THAT WE DON'T ALWAYS DO WHAT IS RIGHT, AND THAT WE OFTEN FEEL COMPELLED TO DO THINGS THAT WE PROBABLY SHOULDN'T DO."

—SCOTT BUCK

Fahy: As the series has progressed, have there been any choices that have been particularly controversial in the writers' room? Was the staff ever divided about the decision to kill Rita, for example? Was there any hesitation over Debra's pseudo-incestuous feelings for Dexter?

Buck: Not necessarily. Those big moments that are controversial are greatly discussed in the writers' room and often with someone playing devil's advocate just to make sure that it is really the right thing to do. But it seems that with all of those bigger moments it was pretty universal in their decision that this was the right way to go for the show.

As for Debra's feeling for Dexter, it just seemed to explain so much about Deb's character, who had one relationship after another with men who seemed on paper to be very good people. She was also clearly someone who had father issues as well. But it made a lot more sense psychologically when it was boiled down to the fact that she had this subconscious love for her brother that went beyond brother/sister love. It made so much sense for the character.

Fahy: It reminds me of that wonderful dream sequence in *Six Feet Under* when Brenda imagines being sexually intimate with her brother Billy—
Buck: Mere coincidence, but I happened to write that episode as well. Someone else brought that up once, and I had completely forgotten about it. So no connection as far as I know.

Fahy: Recently, there has been renewed interest in *The Sopranos* and the way in which the figure of Tony Soprano paved the way for antiheroes on contemporary TV. But it seems to me that whether we're talking about Humbert Humbert or TV figures such as Tony Soprano and Walter White, they all pale in comparison to Dexter Morgan. Dexter seems to be the worst of the worst, the pinnacle of the antihero, because the show asks us to align ourselves and sympathize with a serial killer. Where does the antihero go from here?
Buck: I don't know, because in a way I see him as more sympathetic than someone like Tony Soprano. Tony Soprano knew what he was doing. He could stop what he was doing. He didn't feel this compulsion to hurt people or to kill people; whereas, Dexter—the way

we portray him—simply can't stop himself. He needs to kill almost as much as he needs to breathe. So in a way, there was such an innocence about Dexter , while Tony Soprano was far from innocent. Walter White knows exactly what he is doing every step of the way, and he is purposefully making himself into the baddest guy out there. In a way Dexter is a far more sympathetic character because Tony Soprano and Walter White are more fully realized human beings where Dexter is still struggling to sort of become human in a way. Dexter does have a much greater body count. You have to admit that, and in his own way, he is much more evil and dangerous. But you can also feel sympathy for him that you don't necessarily feel for Tony Soprano or Walter White.

Fahy: When you consider the entire series, where do you think the show stands on the nature vs. nurture issue? Dexter and his brother (whatever their differences) end up in the same place—as serial killers. Hannah can't escape her own need to kill. Lumen returns to her life. Are we all doomed to follow our inherent natures?

Buck: I'm not sure because we sort of walk both sides of that line. We certainly know that he and his brother went through the same circumstances and became these serial killers. But their upbringing was so incredibly different, and that had a huge effect on who Dexter became. No one cares for his brother. No one likes Brian because he is purely evil; whereas, we care for Dexter and might actually think of him as a good person with his own set of morals. That is wholly because of nurture, because of the way Harry raised him.

On the other hand, Hannah doesn't want to kill. For her, killing is always a last resort, but she doesn't have to kill in the way that Dexter does. She kills to make her life easier, to solve problems. And Lumen was horribly damaged and reacted out of the situation. Once she progressed past that, I don't think she has any violent tendencies left in her. Because of what happened to her and because of the trauma, this was her way out of it. If she had not met Dexter, she never would have done the things she did.

Dexter Morgan (Michael C. Hall)—a forensic blood splatter analyst for the Miami-Metro Police Department—gets his hands dirty on and off the job (Showtime). "Seeing Red" (Season 1, Episode 10). Showtime/Photofest, © Showtime.

Fahy: Parenthood is also an integral part of Dexter's character (as a father and stepfather). What is the show trying to say about parenthood? For instance, do you think Dexter is a good parent? Is he a better parent than his father?

Buck: It is difficult to say. His own father—rather than taking him to a psychiatrist for help—shapes him into what he is. But as we learn throughout the final season, it is more complicated than that. Harry did try to do everything to essentially help Dexter. As for Dexter, he is trying to be the very best kind of father he possibly can. This role feels a little out of his wheelhouse—this sort of caring and taking care of someone—and he constantly questions whether he is the best person to do this. But ultimately I think we all agree—at least I certainly do—that he is a good father, the best father that he can be to Harrison.

For our final season, we wanted to move the character forward, but it also felt fun to bring out something new from Dexter's past that no one knew about yet, that there was one more secret about Dexter and about how he was created. So we find out that there was this mother figure (Dr. Vogel) who sort of led Harry along and helped him through this for her own complicated reasons.

Fahy: Well, you may not have imagined yourself as a horror writer, but you have certainly been immersed in the genre for several years. One of the challenges of being a horror writer is balancing the audience's desire for familiar conventions with something new. How do you keep it fresh as a writer?

Buck: For me, it was all about Dexter being a very new character that had not really been seen before. So it was all about approaching the writing through the psychology of discovering who this person is and going on that personal journey with him as he sort of progresses through various stages of evolvement through eight years. The horror accompanied him, but it was always just purely character-based, from my perspective.

Fahy: What do you think are some of the biggest pitfalls in horror writing?

Buck: Falling into convention. There is such an established milieu of horror out that it is hard not to just keep borrowing from things that we've already seen before. If it is not moving the genre forward in some way, it is not particularly interesting.

Fahy: What is the best criticism that you have received as a writer?

Buck: Oh gosh . . . I've received a lot of criticism. (laughs)

I almost want to twist the question around somewhat and say that all the criticism I have received has been helpful. The key is listening to it and not being hurt or insulted by it. And also it is important to judge whether it is valid or not because not all criticism is good. But it's learning how to judge where it comes from. If you don't quite believe the criticism, there still may be some little kernel of truth to it that might suggest you take a step back and look at your work from a slightly different perspective. I do try to listen to what everybody says about my work, and along the way, it has always been very, very helpful—especially with TV writing. It is such a collaborative process, so you constantly have other people to bounce your thoughts off of and to read the pages you've written. For me, it is not one piece of criticism, but collectively it is to listen to what others—whose opinion you value—have to say.

Part II

SEX, LIES, AND VAMPIRES

True Blood

AN INTERVIEW WITH ALEXANDER WOO

Alexander Woo never spent much time thinking about vampires before becoming a staff writer on HBO's *True Blood*. His first job as a television writer began with *Wonderfalls*, but prior to that, he had been a playwright. He attended the Yale School of Drama, and some of his plays have been produced in North Carolina, San Francisco, and Los Angeles. Although he still tries to find time to write plays, television writing has become his passion.

Fahy: You have been a writer and producer on *True Blood* for six years. Prior to this, did you ever imagine that you would have spent so much time thinking about vampires and supernatural?

Woo: Never. (laughs) It happened to be a project that was hiring writers when I was unemployed. My previous show had just been canceled, so it was kind of a lucky stroke for me—and I guess for the other writers as well—that we were available when they were hiring. My background is in theater, so my approach to everything regardless of genre is to base it in characters, to protect the characters. So whether the genre is a horror show like *True Blood*—a Gothic, Southern, romance adventure—or something like my previous show *Sleeper Cell* about Islamic fundamentalists—which is, by the way, equally scary—I still want it rooted in character and to make these characters believable and three-dimensional.

Fahy: Even though your involvement with *True Blood* was a good fit for you at the time, did you have any interest in horror prior to it? Had there been any horror films or books that you particularly enjoyed, that made you think, "I can do this; I can tell a vampire story"?

Woo: I have to admit that I didn't. (laughs)

Films are not really a perfect analog for what we are trying to do with *True Blood* anyway. To me, the experience of watching television is analogous to a long-term relationship between friends. So the relationship between viewers and the characters is like a friendship. I love referring to this piece that the late David Rakoff did on *This American Life* in 2007. He referenced a medical study where the brain chemicals that are fired by watching episodic television are identical to the brain chemicals that are fired by having actual friends. It is emotionally the same experience! And anecdotally you know it to be true. The times when a show has really gotten under your skin you are happy for the characters when good things happen to them. You are angry with them if they do something that makes you mad. You fear for their welfare if they're in danger. And you talk about them with your actual friends the day afterwards as though they were real people. It's an ongoing experience unlike a film which is close-ended in that you can immediately dissect it and talk about the craft of it and the cinematography and the writing. When you are truly immersed in a television series, you feel that you are in this ongoing relationship with characters. In point of fact, I probably see my favorite TV characters more often than I see my actual friends. (laughs) Many of my actual friends I don't see more than once a week. On TV, here they come into my house. They reveal their deepest, darkest secrets. It's a very intimate experience. You are usually watching it alone or with one other person. It's very much like a friendship. The suspension of disbelief is very powerful.

The actors on our shows have reported very much the same thing. When they are approached by fans, it is as though these actors were familiar to them. Even if you intellectually understand these are actors on a screen reciting lines, emotionally you feel this is a journey you are going on with a friend of yours. So it's different in a way from a movie which feels more like a single emotional event where you and two hundred other people in a movie theater are experiencing something gigantic and monumental together. Then it's over. You're let off the hook. You don't wonder what is going to happen to the characters. They don't really live on much. It is the same with a stage play by the way. I had a professor who did an anthropological study of the curtain call, and he suggested—and I think there is a lot of truth to this—that part of the experience of a curtain call is providing a cathartic feeling that goes along with the realization that it is over. We're just actors. We all like each other. We're not really dead. It gives a splash of water to the face, but television doesn't really do that. You are still ensconced in it at the end of an episode. Someone much more academic than I can do a study of how most of the time the main titles for a television series are at the very beginning rather than the end because at the end you want to feel as if you are still immersed in this, as if it is not over.

This is a very long way of answering, but the emotional experience of watching a horror movie is not exactly analogous to the emotional experience of watching a television series in the same genre because it is the difference between a single, very intense emotional event and an ongoing, very intense emotional relationship between the viewer and characters.

"TO ME, THE EXPERIENCE OF WATCHING TELEVISION IS ANALOGOUS TO A LONG-TERM RELATIONSHIP BETWEEN FRIENDS."

—ALEXANDER WOO

Fahy: This idea of comparing the emotional experience of watching television to a relationship makes me think of relationships people have with their favorite shows through technology. In the time you have been writing for television, the experience of watching television has changed radically because of the Internet—through fan sites, social media, Twitter, et cetera. This technology has helped build a much broader and more immediate community for shows like *True Blood*. How has this technology impacted your thinking about television and the way you write for TV?

Woo: I think it certainly helps the success of *True Blood*. The first series I ever worked on was called *Wonderfalls* in 2003, which had sort of a cult following. I firmly believe that if it had premiered in 2007 it would have done a lot better because at the time there wasn't the same infrastructure on the Internet for fans to create a community around it and for it to be popularized in the same way *True Blood* did. We owe a great deal to these fan sites and to the fans who have created communities around it. What it does to us as writers is that we realize television is not disposable the way it once was: it doesn't just air once and no one ever sees it again. Now television is viewed over and over again. It is analyzed and critiqued very carefully by people who are heavily invested in it. This dynamic creates more responsibility for writers to make sure that the story and the characters have structural integrity, that they are frustrating and interesting and compelling and as thoroughly thought-out as possible because people are going to be talking about it for a long time in ways that weren't possible just a few years ago.

Fahy: For you, is the immediacy of this response by fans somewhat analogous to your experiences with live theater—where you have an audience responding in real time to what is happening on stage? I mean, now that you're writing for television at a time when audiences can respond to it as it is airing or blog about immediately afterwards, does this raise the stakes for you (no pun intended for a vampire show)? Or do you view television and theater as completely different beasts?

Woo: (laughs) There are things that are very similar. I hadn't thought of it in the same way because when a show is shot it is several weeks and sometimes several months before it's viewed by the public. The moments that are closest to live theater happen when we are shooting a scene in front of a crew. The crew has gotten so emotionally invested with the show and with the characters that when we shoot the scene you feel them getting involved in it. That has happened a few times on our show where it feels like there is a live performance going on. And maybe the most jaded people of all, which is our crew who work sixteen, eighteen, twenty hours a day, are pulled into it completely. They know these actors personally, but suddenly that suspension of disbelief takes hold and they feel that the event is actually happening in front of them. That is *very* satisfying, and that is very close for me emotionally to live theater.

Fahy: Do you ever find working with source material—in this case Charlaine Harris's novels—restricting? Are you struggling to stay true to the novels while still creating a space for your own originality?

Woo: I think Alan Ball made a very conscious decision at the beginning of the series to start the television show from the same germ as the book series, but from there, even though they sprout from the same seed, they would grow independently of each other. The first season is quite close to the book especially with Sookie's story. But the books are all narrated from Sookie's point of view, and our show is an ensemble show. We have a lot of other characters— a *huge* number of characters –each with their own storylines, so those we have to create completely on our own. As we have moved farther and farther away, there are things in the television series that directly contradict things in the book series. I think fans of both have to be able to compartmentalize one from the other because the show has taken on its own life.

One of the great things about television is that it is a story that evolves as it is being told. If a story wants to go in a certain direction, you can honor that. As we were shooting the first season, one of the things that became very clear was that the character of Lafayette was one that this world wanted to be with. In the book series, he is a

Bill Compton (Stephen Moyer), Eric Northman (Alexander Skarsgård), and Nora Gainesborough (Lucy Griffiths) reveal their fangs in *True Blood* (HBO). "Turn! Turn! Turn!" (Season 5, Episode 1). HBO/Photofest, © HBO.

dead body in a car at the beginning of the second book. The story we were telling did not want to go in that direction. We had the liberty to do that. This was a deliberate choice on Alan Ball's part—to allow this show to evolve on its own rather than staying completely true to the books. There are fans of the books that have protested bitterly about how different the television series is. I personally think that if it was a blow-by-blow reenactment of everything that happens in the book that there is no room for surprise. On an intellectual level, it might satisfy a fan of the book to see something that they have loved and enjoyed come to life, but ultimately in the long run—and this has been a very long run for over six or seven years—if you know exactly what is going to come, it becomes a reenactment of events you already know instead of a relationship with characters who are in your lives. But part of the feeling of being friends with someone is *not* knowing what is going to happen next. And that is the dynamic we are creating on the show.

Fahy: And, as you said, if we see television as having a relationship with the characters on-screen, seeing something predictable would ring false somehow.

Woo: Right. It's a very, very fragile illusion. It can break for someone very quickly with one false move, and then suddenly the illusion is shattered. When that happens, people often disconnect from the show. They stop watching. They stop watching because the characters are doing things they didn't believe. This happens a lot. This has happened to me. It has happened to probably any fan of any television series. You're immersed in it, and suddenly it goes in a direction that completely breaks the illusion for you. Then you lose interest.

Fahy: Is there a particular storyline or character or set of relationships on *True Blood* that you particularly enjoy writing?

Woo: Because of the style of the show, I have always enjoyed when things can get a little more baroque and a little funnier. For me those are the most enjoyable moments. I particularly like the characters that can go there a little more. I love Lafayette. I love Russell Edgington. I love Jason and Andy for those reasons. I also enjoy this because we have enormously gifted actors who can really bring that to life. That is great fun for me. But I want to take care of all of the characters and keep them as true to life as possible. Jessica—even though she isn't necessarily a comedic character—is an emotional center of the show for us, and to keep her emotionally three-dimensional is a priority.

But ultimately, I want to be surprised. It is often one of the most satisfying moments as a writer when you surprise yourself, when a story goes in a direction that is completely organic yet unexpected. So planning it too much in advance is kind of like going on a first date and naming your children. You *can* do it, but chances are things are going to go in a million different directions before you ever get there.

Fahy: And chances are if you're doing that on a first date there probably won't be a second one.

Woo: (laughs) There might not be a second one. We're probably past the first date stage here six years in, but anytime you plan completely for the future, it doesn't tend work out that way.

> "PLANNING [A STORY] TOO MUCH IN ADVANCE IS KIND OF LIKE GOING ON A FIRST DATE AND NAMING YOUR CHILDREN."
>
> —ALEXANDER WOO

Fahy: In recent years, vampires have become fairly common on television and film. What is it about vampire mythology that makes them so popular? Why are people so drawn to it?

Woo: It's a good question, and the fact that it is asked again and again and again suggests there isn't a single answer to it. It is different things to different people. There is something about the forbidden. There is certainly something sexy about it. There is an element of danger and an allegory of the other which resonates with just about everyone. Everyone has felt excluded in one way or another and has felt fear for others or been the target of fear from others. All of these things resonate, but I think it is different things for different people. There isn't probably a single answer.

Fahy: Well, you may not have imagined yourself as a horror writer, but you have certainly been immersed in the genre for several years. It seems that one of the challenges of the genre is both tapping into familiar conventions and keeping it fresh. How do you keep it fresh as a writer?

Woo: I think part of the way that we have kept it fresh on *True Blood* comes from the fact that a lot of us do not come from huge horror backgrounds. This is sort of new territory for a lot of us. Frankly, a lot of those conventions come out of movies, and they don't apply as easily to television. The bloodier, gorier elements of the genre in movies and books need to be adapted for television as it is a different experience. Because of the nature of serial television, we don't have as many pitfalls as if we were making a vampire movie, for instance.

Fahy: And what do you consider to be some of the biggest pitfalls of horror writing?
Woo: Anything you've seen a million times before.

Fahy: You mean if it's too predictable because it's too familiar?
Woo: Yes. If the conventions are too familiar, then you'd have to ask yourself, "Why don't I just turn on my favorite vampire movie? Why didn't I just watch *Interview with a Vampire* or *Dracula* or whatever my favorite vampire movie is instead of watching this show?" Frankly, we have much more time in this television series. This story that we have told now has played for over seventy hours, which is certainly longer than any movie or any book. So we have gotten to explore a good deal deeper. If all we did was biting and staking and killing, I think the experience of watching *True Blood* would be very wearying. Instead, we spend a great deal of time exploring the psychologies of these characters which you don't necessarily have the time to do in a film.

Fahy: What has been the best criticism you have ever received as a writer?
Woo: Wow, I've never been asked that question. I honestly don't have an answer. I don't recall anything anyone has said one way or another. Possibly the reason why is that on a television series you are trying to work together as a group as opposed to as an individual writer. While we each have our own episodes and we handcraft them and we try to make them as good as we can, we are still

writing as a unit. You can't stray too far from the vocabulary of what has been established. Otherwise, again, you're breaking the illusion there. I could write the most brilliant episode of *True Blood* in iambic pentameter, but it would never get past anyone else because that is not the show. That is not the way it is done. In a way, a lot of your own individuality as a writer has to be subsumed to the voice of the show as a whole, which all the writers together create. That might be why I have so much difficulty answering that question in regard to any sort of individual criticism I've gotten on *True Blood*.

Fahy: Do you ever miss writing for live theater and the autonomy that offers as a writer?

Woo: Yes. I still continue to do live theater, but not nearly as much as I used to. Television—especially a show like *True Blood*—can be all-consuming. There is literally no time to do anything else. So I do miss that.

It's a very different experience doing theater, and when I can, I try to go back and do it. Unfortunately, for a lot of playwrights in my generation, theater became increasingly unsustainable. Commercial theater had been moving toward "museum theater"—you find the most famous play you can by the most famous playwright you can, and you get a couple of movie stars to be in it and that is your season. It became more and more difficult for playwrights to find places to have new work done and certainly to make a living doing it. You couldn't earn any sort of income, so you couldn't get your work performed unless you were independently, fabulously wealthy, which most of us were not. Television became a place where suddenly good work was being done, and there was a migration of playwrights—starting in the mid-1990s, through the early 2000s—who came to television because this was suddenly an exciting field. It was no longer the "idiot box." I sort of came in at the tail end of that. I don't know if I was cognizant of it at the time, but I was experiencing the same thing as a lot of playwrights at the time. It was hard to get any work done, and even if you could get it done, you would've spent years getting that work done for a couple thousand dollars, which was not going to pay your rent.

Now, I don't know what compelled Alan Ball to want to hire me. (laughs) I'm very glad he did. The writing sample he read was a stage play of mine. There was probably an affinity to having another playwright on the staff, and he had a couple of playwrights on the staff. I was certainly glad just to have the job. But for whatever reason—and maybe it is because we both had backgrounds in the theater—he decided to take a chance on me.

Fahy: Was there a certain moment in your life when you realized you wanted to be a writer?

Woo: I don't know if there was any single moment because I've always found great joy in the act of writing something and great joy in collaborating with others in seeing a piece of writing come to life. Prior to being a playwright, I had been trained as a fiction writer, which is also a very different experience. In writing fiction, the words you write on the page are the end product itself. In theater and consequently in television (this is not an original idea; I'm cribbing from Michael Frayn here), the script of a play is the blueprint for an event, which is the work itself. I like to call it sheet music. It doesn't sing until someone plays it. That experience of having actors, directors, designers, and a whole team of people bringing one thing to life is a really satisfying experience for me.

Buffy the Vampire Slayer and Battlestar Galactica

AN INTERVIEW WITH JANE ESPENSON

Jane Espenson began her television career as a sitcom writer, and though she made the shift to dramatic writing when she joined the staff of *Buffy the Vampire Slayer* in 1998, the show's humor greatly appealed to her. As she explained to me, "What I like is heart and emotion and comedy. Horror does not exist independent of those." Since the series finale of *Buffy the Vampire Slayer*, Espenson has worked on a diverse range of shows, including *Battlestar Galactica*, *Caprica*, *Torchwood*, and *Once Upon a Time*. She is also the co-creator, producer, and writer of the comedy webseries *Husbands*.

Fahy: You began your television-writing career in science fiction and comedy. How did you first get into horror? Were you interested in the genre before joining *Buffy the Vampire Slayer* or is this something you began to explore more intensely after you started writing for that show?

Espenson: I really don't think of myself as a horror writer or someone with a particular interest in horror. What I like is heart and emotion and comedy. Horror does not exist independent of those. I loved *Buffy* because it was funny and because it had big ideas. And it was a combination of genres and styles. If you look at the title itself, *Buffy the Vampire Slayer*, you see comedy, horror, action. Horror is just part of it. It just came along as part of the ride.

Fahy: Once you entered the world of *Buffy*, you spent a lot of time thinking about vampires. For you, what aspects of the vampire mythology were you most interested in playing with as a writer?

Espenson: I think there is something inherently sexy about vampires as has been remarked on many times—the biting, the overpowering nature, the siring, and such—and there is this sense of succumbing to the seduction of a vampire that is very interesting. But they are also really funny. Here are these powerful creatures with hysterical vulnerabilities like sunlight. That is a fairly funny vulnerability because it's everywhere. Take drinking blood. There is something so funny about blood as one's natural beverage. (laughs) There is just a lot of humor in the mythology maybe because vampires have been around for long. Maybe I see humor because I don't find vampires genuinely horrifying. Aging is genuinely horrifying— that scene in the movie where you look in the mirror and see your teeth fall out and see your body as old, where the monster that has got your mother's face, where *The Exorcist* kind of thing happens. That stuff is genuinely horrifying. I find vampires sort of comedo-horrifying. They don't strike fear in my heart, and that doesn't make them strictly horror for me. They are certainly very, very good literary devices that can help you tell a story because of the metaphorical ways you can use them.

Fahy: Given your interest in the funnier aspects of vampires, are you sometimes surprised by television shows and films that take the vampire mythology so seriously, that lack the kind of humor that was so pervasive on *Buffy*?

Espenson: Yes, I think it does. Obviously, people have succeeded. There have been multiple franchises post-*Buffy* that have been very successful. The first couple did surprise me. I sort of felt like, "Didn't we do that? Didn't Joss [Whedon] cover that?" But when you pick up the *Twilight* books, you realize they're just doing something very different with it. They are tapping into the romanticism of it. The romanticism is a very potent part of the mythology. The sex metaphor of the vampire is very potent and alive. That makes sense. Some people have found a way to make vampires very scary,

A tennis racket will do. Buffy Summers (Sarah Michelle Gellar) battles vampires and the forces of darkness in *Buffy the Vampire Slayer* (WB). "The Freshman" (Season 4, Episode 1). Photofest.

to dig them up out of the ground and re-fang them, so to speak, to make them tap into the things that genuinely scare us.

And loss of control. Loss of control is very scary. That is probably my greatest fear. My nightmares are: "I'm in a car and can't steer it." That kind of thing. I think there is a way to make vampires be very potent in that way. They make you lose control of yourself, and that is very frightening.

Fahy: In hindsight, what were the most valuable lessons that you learned as a writer from *Buffy the Vampire Slayer*—particularly in terms of the art of creating suspenseful narratives, maintaining story arcs, and developing characters?

Espenson: Well, Joss Whedon is a master of all those things, and I learned as much as I could but not nearly as much as he has to offer. One of the things he emphasized is the importance of building your story around a theme, around what you are trying to say. Don't just come up with a story and then ask yourself, "What theme does this illustrate?" Joss would genuinely start from the question, "What is the thing that I want to say? What is something I sincerely believe and how do I build the story around it?" Very few people do that because that takes a huge amount of discipline and faith that you really have something to say. I don't know that everybody does.

Another important thing is keeping an eye on your main character and making sure that they are the hero of the story, that they are the one going through the emotional journey. On the show, we used to ask, "What's the Buffy of it?" And this is something Joss alums always talk about. If you brought in a story and it was all great and it had these great moves and it was shocking and it was exciting and it had something to say but Buffy wasn't going on a journey, you were going to get the question, "What's the Buffy of it?" I think that is really important for any show—to have that sense for the arc of your main character.

Joss sort of took the basic nuts and bolts of structure for granted and then elaborated on them. So for him, the show never went in the expected direction. He knew how to take the expected direction, but he would embroider it in some way. You would have the classic act break but with some kind of twist. We had one with Ethan Rayne, the villain for that episode, in which he was standing alone and saying, "Oh, you have no idea what's in store for you." And Giles suddenly walks into the room, totally ruining his villain moment. Then Ethan would say, "Oh, bugger it. I thought you'd gone." (laughs) We always tried building to the great moment that will always work and not just letting that be enough. We wanted to find the variation on it that was funny or shocking or horrifying.

Fahy: You mention Ethan, and that reminds me of your first episode for the series, "Band Candy," in which the adults of Sunnydale start acting like teenagers after eating candy bars. Along the lines of what you have been talking about, what were you trying to say with that episode?

Espenson: That is an interesting one because so many of the episodes were Joss's idea. That episode is one that I did bring in from outside and pitch. I pitched that at my job interview actually. When I pitched it, it was a coffee shop. It wasn't the candy causing this adult behavior, but candy makes much more sense, though. The idea was that as teenagers—at one time or another—we all think that if our parents could just remember what it would be like to be teenagers, if our parents could be more like us, everything would be better. The horror comes from when they do remember and from recognizing that we do need our parents to be parents, even if we resent it sometimes. It's very frightening when they are not there. Your parents out-of-control is, in a way, worse than you out-of-control. That was the idea I brought in that Joss responded to.

And it was really fun getting to write Joyce and Giles as if it was their show. We didn't have a lot of scenes that were just Joyce and Giles in the series, and they have a number of scenes in that episode. Giving the adults equal time was really fun, and playing with the idea not just of them being teenagers now but of them being teenagers then was really fun. I got to play with what their cultural references would have been. All Giles's musical tastes were from Joss. Joss supplied that stuff. And Joyce's references and Principal Snyder's references were sort of more the American teen experience, and that was definitely coming from me.

> "THERE IS SOMETHING I LOVE ABOUT TAKING SECONDARY OR TERTIARY CHARACTERS AND PUTTING THEM AT THE MIDDLE OF AN EPISODE BECAUSE IN REAL LIFE THERE ARE NO SIDEKICKS. IN REAL LIFE EVERYBODY IS THE HERO OF THEIR OWN STORY."
>
> —JANE ESPENSON

Fahy: You seemed to enjoy writing for the character Jonathan and his friends—from Jonathan appearing in the watchtower at school with a rifle in "Earshot" to his role in "Conversations with Dead People." What appealed to you about that group of guys? Why did you enjoy writing for them so much?

Espenson: Yes, I loved writing for the trio—and for Jonathan before the trio—because they are funny. There is something I love about taking secondary or tertiary characters and putting them at the middle of an episode because in real life there are no sidekicks. In real life everybody is the hero of their own story. So I think it is always valid to write an episode of television where you take a character that has always been on the periphery and point out that for them it is *not* the periphery. For them, this is life. A secondary or tertiary character is often a very funny character because they have been drawn to this point with broader strokes, so they often have something very comedic about them. For instance, Andrew's episode, "Storyteller," played off his tendency to dramatize the events around him and to frame everything as a narrative. That is a very funny trait that would play out really well when you put it center stage. I like a novelty episode of television. At the time, those types of episodes don't always get a lot of attention, but when you look back on them, you see something really special. What is the episode of *Star Trek* that everyone remembers? Probably "The Trouble with Tribbles."

Fahy: When you wrote "After Life" at in the beginning of the sixth season (after Buffy is killed and witchcraft brings her back from the dead), the series took a very dark turn. Were there any debates in the writers' room about that darker direction, about her relationship with Spike?

Espenson: Yes, the show did get darker. There were never debates in the room because TV shows are not democracies. Joss is the author of a novel, and we were helping him write the chapters. The character and the story went in that dark direction very naturally. Here is this young person who is fighting these fights every week, so you have to ask: What kind of future does she have? How was she ever going to be able to lay down the stake and move on? How are these incredibly trying experiences affecting her? If you treat the characters as real people and if you give them that much darkness, there is going to be some darkness accumulating in their lives. So it was very, very natural. I think it would have felt forced if she had sort of breezily gone on. I think the show would have felt repetitive, and I don't think it would have felt genuine any longer. So the turn toward darkness wasn't like all of us in the room were getting depressed. We were all very happy. (laughs) It was a natural direction for the characters. As we made Buffy overcome bigger and bigger challenges, it put her through more and more of all that crap one goes through on that way to overcoming great challenges. Darkness occurs.

I wrote an episode called "Doublemeat Palace," which was a very silly one but also a very dark one. It was both simultaneously. At the time, it was I'd say the least beloved *Buffy* episode ever. Now, I think it is looked back on with some fondness. I like the way it was darkly funny. She was working in fast food, and the episode gave the feeling that this may be her life, this may be her future. It is in a weird place with weird people and a weird mystery. There was something atmospheric about it. She was sort of seeing Spike but not really. I thought it really captured that turn toward darkness but in a way that showed that it wasn't <u>not</u> going to be entertaining.

Fahy: Is there an episode of *Buffy* that you wrote that you feel best typifies what the series was trying to do?

Espenson: I really like "Harsh Light of Day," and that is the one where Buffy sleeps with a guy in college. Spike is getting the Gem of Amarra, so he can be out in the daylight. I feel that almost every single scene in that episode had someone yearning at the same time that it was very funny. Every single scene in that one had something deeply emotional in it. I also really like "Pangs" (the Thanksgiving one), "Superstar," and I really like "Storyteller"—the sort of novelty episodes.

I was very fortunate on that show to be assigned to a lot of episodes that were fun. But every episode of *Buffy* was a joy to write. There aren't really a lot of clunkers. The Thanksgiving episode was an idea Joss had been playing with for a long time, maybe even pre-*Buffy*. He wanted to do a Thanksgiving episode that really played with the actual history of Thanksgiving, which is horrific. Here is this great, fun celebration that is rooted in all this blood. So I had a couple of days during the writing of that episode where I was able to take the time to drive up the coast and visit some museums that housed Chumash artifacts and talk to some people of Chumash descent. I probably went to three or four spots and talked with people and did a bunch of reading. So I educated myself about that history. I didn't know much about it then, so I had to learn about it during the two weeks I had to write the episode.

For sheer horror, the episode that feels most horrific is called "Same Time, Same Place," where Willow has that monster sitting on her and pulling her skin off in strips. That one has some good old sheer horror in it. That episode was about being out-of-sync with all of your friends and feeling detached from the rest of life. So it was about something real and horrific, and it was captured in a horrific way. Joss was really good about making sure that the episodes were about the heart of the show. So it is difficult to find an episode that doesn't typify what the show was about.

Fahy: One of your earliest scripts was for *Star Trek: Deep Space Nine*, so as a science fiction fan, was the opportunity to work on *Battlestar Galactica* a dream come true? And had you been a fan of the original show?

Espenson: I had probably watched a couple of episodes of the original one when I was a young teen, but it hadn't really been one of my go-to shows. I loved *Star Trek*. That was my real sci-fi obsession. I used to pitch at *Star Trek: Next Generation* a number of years before I wrote that *Star Trek: Deep Space Nine* episode that you referenced. That was really a dream come true. *Battlestar* hadn't been an obsession of mine. I don't think having it be an obsession of yours is a great prerequisite for liking the remake. They are so different in tone. A friend—Drew Greenberg, who was on *Buffy* with me— recommended *Battlestar* as a show I might like. After *Buffy*, a lot of us spent a couple of seasons casting around and wondering, "What do I want to do? What is going to be as good as *Buffy*?" It was hard to find something. I started watching *Battlestar* and recognized that this is that good. This is really something extraordinary. I knew Ron because I used to pitch to him at *Star Trek: Next Generation*, so I was able to call and to see if he remembered me and to get a meeting with him at *Battlestar*. That turned into a couple of freelance episodes in season three and then a full-time gig in season four.

Fahy: Several of your episodes focused on Gaius Baltar's cult. What drew your interest in writing about that cult and the cult mentality more broadly?

Dr. Gaius Balter (James Callis) struggles with his inner demons in Battlestar Galactica (Syfy). Also shown is Number Six (Tricia Helfer). "Final Cut" (Season 2, Episode 8). Photographer: Carole Segal. Syfy Channel/Photofest, © Syfy.

Espenson: Again, you are sort of assigned to an episode more than deciding, "I'm going to write this one over here." But I was so happy to get those episodes because I love Baltar's character. I love the humor in *Battlestar*, and it is an aspect of the show that doesn't get enough credit for being as funny a show as it is and much of that is Baltar. I am fascinated by cults. Maybe again it is the visceral nature of the loss of control. That you are handing your control over to somebody else and how did they make that happen? Absolutely fascinating. I was really proud of a line I took in one of those episodes. The thing that Baltar says that is so dangerous is to tell people they're perfect. Of course, that is the most seductive message in the world. Wait, I don't have to change anything. I don't have to work. I don't have to think. I'm perfect just like I am. It sounds like such a positive message, but it is the most destructive thing in the world because it is telling people to turn off their ability to improve themselves. And, of course, it sends the message, "Listen to me because I'm the one saying the thing that you always hoped to hear." I just loved the dichotomy of that: it is beautiful and terribly dangerous.

That phrase that you hear sometimes—"emotional vampire"—is a really good one. There are people out there who are emotional vampires, and they take energy by draining you of your life force. You can definitely see cult leaders of a certain type being like that. That is where they get their strength and you lose yours.

Fahy: I wanted to shift to more writerly questions. What was the first television show that made you want to be a TV writer? What appeals to you about television writing as opposed to other genres?
Espenson: I watched a lot of TV as a kid, and there were a lot of shows where I would write a story in my head for them. *Barney Miller* was definitely one of them. *Welcome Back Cotter* was one of them. *The Love Boat* . . . I would think of little stories for *The Love Boat* all the time! Probably of all the shows that I watched, the one that was most influential for me was *M*A*S*H* because *M*A*S*H* is the one where I actually sat down and tried to write an episode when I was a kid. That was the one that seemed attainable because I had read an article about people submitting scripts to *M*A*S*H*. So that is probably why I did that. It was also a show in which the characters were so well defined that I knew I could write those voices.

Fahy: You said before that you focus more on the emotional context for the characters as opposed to genre, but you are someone who has moved in-between a lot of different genres quite fluidly—science fiction, horror, fantasy. When you are writing in genre fiction, how do you strike that balance between familiar conventions and novelty to keep it fresh?
Espenson: First of all, I want to speak to moving smoothly between genres. If you don't think about the genre, that is a big help in that regard. These are just people. In real life you don't know comedy people and drama people. We all move through our lives, and there are episodes of our lives that are comedic and there are episodes that are tragic. We still react true to ourselves. We don't switch our

personalities for those things. That means that characters exist independently of the genres they live in. If you just think about writing for characters, you don't have to think about genre. That will make the writing smoother. The characters will feel real.

In terms of striking a balance between convention and invention, that is usually the province of the person who is running the show. At the stage in the scriptwriting when you are making those decisions, you are still sitting in the writers' room with seven other people working on it as a group. It sort of emerges from the culture of the show. In all the episodes that have gone before—starting with the pilot episode which the showrunner usually wrote alone—all of those sort of things set the rules for a particular show. So that is in the air that you breathe in the writers' room. You are not making that decision every week about how to address the conventions of the genre while keeping it fresh. That is baked into the culture of the show. And then the viewers get it too. The viewers know what rules an episode of *Supernatural* or *Once Upon a Time* or whatever show lives by. Keeping it fresh is about respecting the characters and letting them live and breathe like real people. The story will be influenced by the characters as much as it is by the genre. That is what will keep the balance.

Fahy: You've been talking about the need not to compartmentalize things in one's writing. One ought not to think exclusively in terms of comedy or drama because that isn't true to life. But it does seem like comedy is a big part of all of your writing and something you enjoy reveling in. Did your passion for comedy inspire your new web series *Husbands*? What are the advantages of producing something online directly?

Espenson: That idea came from Brad Bell, who co-created the show with me. He and I both consider ourselves primarily comedic writers, so he brought me this idea for doing a comedy. The things that appealed to me about it were getting to work with Brad, whom I think is a creative genius, getting to work on flat-out comedy (really pure joke writing, which he and I love), and getting to write something important because of the marriage-equality aspect of the show. I think it was all of those things.

And I absolutely feel there are advantages to producing it online directly. The fact that we are able to write and produce the show as we see it—sort of adhering to Brad's creative vision—is made a lot easier by the fact that there are fewer layers in the process. We can put out the show that we envision, and we are enjoying that a lot. As a side note, I'd add that Brad loves comedy, but the thing he loves more than anything is horror. He knows every beat of every important horror movie. That is his main media joy. (laughs) Maybe there is some conflation between horror and comedy—the same way that math and music live in the same people.

Fahy: What was the best criticism/advice you ever received as a writer?
Espenson: (sigh)

Fahy: Interestingly enough, that question always seems to inspire the same kind of reaction—a deep sigh or exhale.
Espenson: (laughs) That is so funny. I love technical aspects of writing, so my first thought was to talk about how to write dialogue that really sounds natural, which has been a shockingly important part of my career. You can have the best ideas, the best command of structure (far better than mine—I don't consider myself to be particularly good at structure at all), but it is going to sit there on the page like a big, limp, deflated road-kill frog if you don't have the ability to make the characters' language sound fresh and natural. Not too poetic. People don't really talk that way. Not too original that is sounds written, but original enough that is sounds fresh. So finding the way to write really good dialogue is more important than it's given credit for. I think it has been a key to my success, and it's shocking how far that one little ability can take you.

For me, writing dialogue is something that always came naturally, but my training in college as a linguist probably helped a lot with that. Linguistics is about the spoken word, and it's about how people really speak. It's not about the rules of grammar. It's about the utterances that people actually produce. So you think a lot about and listen carefully to how people actually speak. That really helps craft an ear for dialogue.

Part III

ZOMBIES, MONSTERS, AND WEREWOLVES, OH MY

Night of the Living Dead (1968). Directed by George A. Romero. Continental Distributing Inc./Photofest, © Continental Distributing Inc.

Supernatural, The Dead Zone, Miracles, The Gates, and The Mothman Prophecies

AN INTERVIEW WITH RICHARD HATEM

When Richard Hatem is not seeking out haunted vacation spots, he is writing for some of the scariest shows on television. He has not only been a staff writer on shows such as *The Dead Zone*, *Supernatural*, and *Grimm*, but he also created two series—*Miracles* and *The Gates*. Although it seems that Hatem wanted to be a television writer from the first moment he sat in front of the small screen, his career in Hollywood began as a screenwriter, writing two feature films—*Under Siege 2: Dark Territory* and *The Mothman Prophecies*—before moving into television.

Fahy: From your first film *The Mothman Prophecies* to your most recent work as a writer on *Grimm*, you have been interested in supernatural horror stories. How did you first get into horror and what were your earliest influences?

Hatem: Well, I've been interested in the supernatural for as long as I can remember, but it didn't really play a large role in my early writing. A lot of stuff I did in high school and college, when I was writing spec samples for different shows, was more action stuff. I was trying to sell stuff to *The A-Team*, *Remington Steele*, *The Equalizer*, and shows like that. Actually, my first movie, which was co-written with Matt Reeves, was basically *Die Hard* on a train, and it turned into *Under Siege 2: Dark Territory* with Steven Seagal. At that point, I was looked at as an action writer. It wasn't until I came across the book for *The Mothman Prophecies* that I thought: "Maybe there is a way I can take this nonfiction book, which is a grab bag of weird psychic phenomenon with this little thread running through it about the events that occurred in Point Pleasant, and revisit all of that horror stuff I loved." At the time, my approach was different—and it still is different—than the way most supernatural movies go. The whole point behind *The Mothman Prophecies* is that when you deal with questions of a supernatural sort, you really don't get solid answers. In movies, you always do, but I wanted to write a movie where you didn't, which is probably why it didn't do that well. (laughs)

Almost every writer who is my age—I'd say in their forties—tends to mention the same things. We all read Stephen King. I read Stephen King voraciously, and he taught me how to write by basically making it so evident that you had to care about the characters before you were going to care about any of the supernatural stuff that happens to them. First you've got to know them as normal people. Once you completely recognize them and they feel like the people next door, you totally buy it when they are being attacked by vampires. We're not starting on planet Mars. We're starting right here on your own block. That is what made his work so compelling to me.

It's so funny. For thirty years of my life, no one knew any of my references. But I can go on any TV show, sit in a room with the other writers, and mention Carl Kolchak, the Night Stalker, and *every* single person knows exactly who I'm talking about because they were watching that when they were eight years old, too. Suddenly, we were all members of the same club. We all loved those things, and for me, it led to this career.

Fahy: So when you got the chance to work on the television series *The Dead Zone*, was that a dream come true?
Hatem: I'd like to say yes. We knew it was the final season unless something miraculous happened. So the whole new staff that came

on the show knew that we were coming on for the final twelve or thirteen episodes. We were all kind of hoping that Stephen King would make a cameo. Maybe we could meet him and get him to sign our books. But that never happened.

The challenge of writing the fifth season of *The Dead Zone*—and maybe the fifth season of any show—is that really all of the good ideas have been taken. (laughs) So we were really digging through the junk drawer of ideas and trying to fit various parts together. I mean, how many more things can happen in this small, Maine town and to these characters? We also lost a lot of the main characters because of budget cuts. We started the season knowing that a handful of the audience's favorite characters were not going to come back. So we were even more depleted in terms of our storytelling options. Don't get me wrong. The writers' room was fantastic. We were all having a blast, but it was tough to write. Again, the concept was running on fumes at that point.

"I THINK THE AMERICAN PUBLIC TREATS THE HORROR GENRE THE WAY I TREAT THE DESSERT BUFFET. I'M HOPING FOR SOMETHING I LOVE, BUT IF I DON'T FIND IT, I'LL TAKE WHATEVER IS THERE."

—RICHARD HATEM

Fahy: Is there a King story you would *love* to get your hands on and do an adaptation of?

Hatem: That's a great question because he has written so much. Typically, I fall into one or two categories with his books and short stories. Either they are so great that they should not be adapted in any form, ever, and they should just live as what they are. Or they are unadaptable. They are filled with ideas that work because of his voice. He pulls off a lot by voice. You'll read a short story or an entire novel and realize that there isn't really a crackerjack plot at work here. I just love sitting down and hearing Stephen King tell a story. Transferring that material to any other medium immediately creates all sorts of problems and challenges. Now we have to add a plot. Now we have to add act breaks, and all sorts of structural stuff that he doesn't have to do. By doing that, you often lose the charm of what is there. That being said, I will tell you this. *The Dark Half* is a book that has been around and around Hollywood. They made a feature version of it, but people are dying to figure out a way to do that as a TV show, as a miniseries, as a something. That is the one I hear about probably more than any other one of his books. People are just desperate to figure out a way to crack it, and I would not be surprised if you see that either on network or basic cable sometime in the next five years.

On the flip side, there is a lot of stuff out there that I'm just not interested in. I read Stephen King. I used to read Anne Rice, but that's about it for me. I'm not on board with just anything that crawls up out of hell. Obviously, people want stuff, and they tend to prefer good stuff. But if the good stuff is not around, they will often take anything. I think the American public treats the horror genre the way I treat the dessert buffet. I'm hoping for something I love, but if I don't find it, I'll take whatever is there.

For me, when it comes to horror, it breaks down into styles and subgenres. I don't consider a family being trapped in a cabin and watching them get pulverized one by one by insane bikers to be horror. Yes, that is horrifying, but for me it is not horror. I'm interested in the supernatural, so I will always be gravitating more toward things like *The Sixth Sense* rather than *The Hills Have Eyes.*

Fahy: They have a very different approach to where terror comes from—

Hatem: Yes, but a lot of things can inspire terror. You can watch CNN and feel terror, but I also draw a line in terms of definitions. Terror is one thing. Horror is an emotion that is evoked through

Cleopatra (Olga Baclanova) becomes "one of us" the hard way in Tod Browning's *Freaks* (1932). MGM/ Photofest, © MGM.

the uncanny. There has to be a recognition that something isn't following natural laws. For my money, Tod Browning's *Freaks* is a perfect example of this. Even though we are dealing with real people (those were actual people born with diseases and birth defects), it evokes horror because when you're looking at these people, you're recognizing a humanity within them, but the physical form of that humanity is so different from what is considered normal that it evokes horror. You take that a little further into fictional, genre storytelling, and you get movies like *The Thing*. I still think John Carpenter's *The Thing* is a masterpiece. It makes you suspect other people, but when the Thing actually comes out on stage and does its "thing," it is horrifying.

Fahy: Speaking of *Freaks*, that reminds me of a story about F. Scott Fitzgerald when he was working as a screenwriter for MGM. One afternoon at the studio commissary, he inadvertently sat down at a table with two of the stars from Browning's film, the conjoined twins Daisy and Violet Hilton. As soon as he saw them, Fitzgerald ran outside to vomit.

Hatem: (laughs) I love that! I love that story! There has been a lot of talk recently about this concept in animation called the "uncanny valley." It has to do with what sorts of things human beings can accept in terms of animation and what they find appealing. On one end of the spectrum, you've got highly stylized characters that don't look human at all—*The Simpsons* or *Phineas and Ferb.* That is appealing because they are clearly not human. Way over on the other end of the spectrum, you've just got actual human beings, and we recognize them as such. But when you're using animation or computer-generated images to really try to fool audiences into thinking that they are seeing a real person when they're not, the human brain starts to get a little queasy because it knows something is wrong. That is what people in the computer and animation world call the "uncanny valley," which is sort of where you don't want to be because it is no fun. It is actually horrifying. This problem can be seen in films like *The Polar Express* where the character looks kind of like Tom Hanks, but it looks like Tom Hanks fed through some weird sort of filter. And it's disturbing.

What's so funny about this is when I was writing *Mothman* fifteen years ago there was one particular scene where this sort of weird entity named Indrid Cold appears to one of the characters. As he is relating a story, he goes into a flashback of his memory, and in the original script, I described the character Indrid Cold as looking like a parody of a human being, like something that is trying to hold human form but is having trouble doing it. That is what I was going for—capturing the feeling that there was just something not right about this person and that feeling pervades the book *The Mothman Prophecies.* So I was trying to get to that, to a deep sense of wrongness about his human form.

Fahy: It does seem that much of your horror writing deals with elements of the uncanny, particularly through encounters with supernatural forces that exist in a largely hidden or unseen realm (mothmen, ghosts, religious miracles, the Wesen of *Grimm*). Part of the terror in those stories comes from an average person getting a glimpse into this unseen world and trying to make sense of it. What is it about these types of stories (these encounters with supernatural beings or phenomenon) that appeal to you as a storyteller—as opposed to writing stories about serial killers, for instance?

Hatem: For me personally, and this is certainly true as I get older, the serial-killer story loses its appeal as entertainment because serial killers exist. I actually know a person who has lost a family member due to a murderer. I'm not saying you can't tell those stories. I'm just saying it is difficult to find the metaphor in something so real. That, of course, is the trick when you write about anything. How do you find the metaphor in war, the metaphor in disease, the metaphor in the real thing so that you're not just relating a new story or making a documentary? Instead, you're commenting on it from within. Horror allows for that. That is the whole point of it. It allows you to step away from the literalness of an event and explore the feelings of it through the guise of genre storytelling.

I grew up as a kid reading books about Bigfoot and UFOs, and it was always about people telling stories of encounters with whatever. The fun part about those stories is that they have real cool beginnings, great middles, and no endings. Basically, we went camping, we heard something, we went outside, we saw something we can't explain, the end. (laughs) There is no third act. There is no resolution—like, the UFO landed, an alien came out, we went on an adventure, and I made a friend. Or I met a ghost; it led us to his burial place, we dug it up, and discovered that this person had been murdered. The next morning we called in the authorities, and we found the killer. That never happens. It's just something weird (I don't have any way to process it based on what I know about the world), so it just remains a weird thing forever. That is what I love because everything remains a weird thing. Forget the question: Why did that ghost show up? The real questions are more interesting: Why did that relationship end? Why did that friend disappear from my life? Why did that person suddenly get sick and die instead of someone else or me? Those are the questions that haunt us, that literally haunt us. So I can tell a story about a weird event and spend as much time in the question period and as little time as possible in the answer period, and I evoke the feeling that I want to evoke. I think my show *Miracles* did that really well. We always had an answer. It was fun to just deal with the emotional impact of the question.

Fahy: As you're talking about the way horror stories function as metaphors for some of the profound questions that face all of us, another question pops up for me—a little off-topic—but I'm curious given your lifelong interest in supernatural stories. Do you believe in ghosts and supernatural phenomenon?

Hatem: It's kind of a joke. If I ever did see a ghost or a UFO, I'd be the last person anyone would ever believe (laughs)—although Stephen King does believe he saw a ghost at some point. I've never had a supernatural experience. I've gone to psychics and had readings. Some have been wildly inaccurate, and some have been oddly, ridiculously accurate. That is about as close to the supernatural as I have gotten in my real life. Here is where I am with belief. About ten years ago, I was about 90 percent in. I'm like, "Yeah. Afterlife. Ghosts. Everything!" Then I drifted way out, and now I'm about 50/50. I'm reading a lot about near-death experiences and trying to focus on the issue of human consciousness. That is where near-death experience research is right now. They are trying to nail down the question: How are people having vivid mental experiences during a time when there should be no mental activity? So if you can forget about afterlife and heaven and hell and just for a moment answer that question (even if the answer is one that is purely scientific), at least you have further pushed back the boundaries of our definition of human consciousness. That is the biggest question of all.

Fahy: I remember you telling me once that you used to like visiting haunted places, so this shifting focus to human consciousness as opposed to the supernatural sounds like a big change.
Hatem: In some ways, yeah. But if I had the opportunity to go on vacation somewhere, I would definitely try to find a haunted hotel hoping that something would happen.

Fahy: That might make for some bad vacation choices but some interesting things to write about.
Hatem: (laughs) It is kind of funny that you asked that. At the time I was most convinced that there was an afterlife, I was personally going through the end of a marriage. When I look back, I realize that metaphorically I was leaving one life behind and moving on into an unknown realm. It is hard for me to look back at that and not draw a connection between the belief in the survival of the soul and my own mental journey from one existence into another. It felt every bit transformative at that time. As that emotional event receded in the rearview mirror, I moved out of that preoccupation. Now I'm looking at my life in much more stark terms—what is really here and what really isn't. The notion of an afterlife has become more murky for me when we're talking about an afterlife after death.

Fahy: We started out talking about *The Mothman Prophecies*. How did you make the shift from feature film writing to television writing? Was that a conscious choice or had you always been interested in television and writing for television?
Hatem: I started out in high school and college completely wanting to write for television, and not really focusing on film at all. Truly by coincidence, my first sale was a film script, and that sort of dictated my career path for the next five or six years. Then just

as coincidentally, I went into a meeting thinking that it was about rewriting a feature-film script and discovering that the meeting was about taking ideas from that script and creating a television show. On pure interest in the subject matter, I agreed to write a TV pilot—again, not really thinking it would go anywhere because most things don't go anywhere. That project became the series *Miracles*. Once I worked in television and had a bit of momentum there and realized that this is a medium where stuff actually gets produced on a regular schedule, the form itself became so appealing, I stuck around, and I've never regretted it.

But as I said, that passion for TV started much earlier. When I was in middle school and high school, *The Rockford Files* and later *The A-Team* were two shows that I just loved so much. That interest made me aware of Stephen J. Cannell, who co-created, wrote, and imbued those shows with his own voice. That is when I became aware of something really important—the ability to express voice as a TV writer. I think for the generation right after me, *Buffy the Vampire Slayer* is the show that did that. It was genre with a voice. It made people realize that it is not the bare bones of the genre but the voice that interprets the tenets of a genre that makes it so appealing. It made a lot of people say, "Let me take a crack at this." But it was the voice of Stephen Cannell that brought me into the awareness that you could express voice in television.

Fahy: The issue of voice raises some questions for me. One of the shows you worked on after *Miracles* was *Supernatural*, and you were part of this series as a writer and producer for its first season. Particularly in its early seasons, *Supernatural* carried the burden of following *The X-Files*, and the show has always been self-conscious about that—through humorous references to Scully and Mulder and casting decisions. In the writers' room, how did you discuss the issue of being linked with *The X-Files* and needing to be distinct from it?

Hatem: To be fair, I was with *Supernatural* for a very short amount of time, and for me part of talking about *Supernatural* (aside from recognizing its many, many fantastic qualities that have allowed it to exist on television for years) is talking about my utter failure at being able to tell those stories—at least at that time. When I was on that show in the early days (I'm talking about the first six months of production, the first half of the first season), my notion of the show was that it was telling very emotional stories, and I was approaching them from that angle. I would have been much better served to approach them from the perspective of finding the coolest, most fun, action-y approach to urban legends, and let's exploit those, because I think that is what the show does really well. Over the arc of the nine years that it has been on, it has done a great job with emotion starting with those two brothers.

Stepping away from my own experience on the show, I can tell you that there was never any talk of *The X-Files* in the writers' room. That was never the fear. The fear was: How scary can we make this show and still have it be on the air? What will they let us get away with? And what can we deliver? So let's try to deliver scary, but let's not overreach to the point where we try to deliver something and can't quite do it. Let's find a sweet spot where it is still a really scary show, where we are still trading in fear, but we're not biting off more than we can chew. At the same time, we wanted to keep the brothers funny, to keep a certain amount of pep in the show.

Fahy: To me, *Supernatural* is somewhat unique in focusing on two brothers (as opposed to a romantic relationship), muscle cars, and rock 'n' roll. My initial connection with the show came from the fact that I have a younger brother (so I got the sibling dynamic), and my first car was a 1967 Plymouth Barracuda, which I had for thirteen years. My brother's first car was a 1956 Plymouth Firebird, so we were a family of old cars and brothers. So that was fun, but at the time part of me wondered if the show would appeal to people without those experiences.

Hatem: That is 100 percent Eric Kripke. He may not get enough credit for the degree to which that show is about his life—the

The Winchester brothers, Sam (Jared Padelecki) and Dean (Jensen Ackles), are on the run in *Supernatural* (WB). "Pilot" (Season 1, Episode 1). Photographer: Justin Lubin. WB Television/Photofest, © WB Television.

arguments over whose cassette gets to go into the cassette player on a road trip. That is absolutely drawn from his experiences growing up and his family life. He brought that to the show, which is a giant part of its appeal and its genius. That was all very intentional and autobiographical.

Fahy: To shift to more writerly questions, as you know, horror fans seem to crave both novelty and the familiar, and in one of your more recent shows, *The Gates*, you incorporated vampires and witches and a whole assortment of supernatural figures—each with their own distinct mythologies and legacies. How did you try to keep it fresh as a writer on that show?

Hatem: For me, what was cool about *The Gates*—above and beyond anything else—was the level to which the stories worked metaphorically. From a concept on up, it felt like we could tell stories for a hundred years. It is basically about people trying to hide aspects of who they are from their friends and neighbors. (laughs) So it was *Desperate Housewives*, but the woman with the drinking problem is drinking too much blood. To me, that is a secret worth keeping, and their lives literally depend on it. Outside of that, it was a show not about monsters embracing their monstrosity but really trying to hide it. That is what we all do. We all walk around with things that we think make us monsters that we try to hide from other people. Maybe we are hiding aspects of our political views or our lack of compassion for people who are suffering on the other side of the world or our lack of morality or nobility. We are all hiding those things, and that is what all the main characters on *The Gates* were doing, which made them so sympathetic and so horrifying because every once in a while we saw them indulge in their "worst sides" and we saw them deal with the consequences of that. That felt very familiar. Sometimes we just blow up at our spouse and say things that we regret. We let the monster out, and then we have to deal with the result of that. From a purely storytelling point of view, that interested me forever.

When it came to actually doing the show, many of our creative decisions in terms of the monsters were dictated by what we were able to do. For instance, there were werewolves—people who turned into werewolf creatures—but early on we realized we were never going to be able to do makeup or CGI effects to achieve a quasi-human wolf image. So at a certain point, we decided that they were not werewolves. They were wolves. That is what they turned into. So in one shot, they are a person and in the next shot there is a wolf in the frame, running on all fours down the street. (laughs) We're just going to have to embrace that as our mythology and move on. We faced a similar issue with the vampires. Are we only going to see these characters at night? No. We decided that in our world they have figured out a way to cook up a sunscreen that works for them. Every morning, they put on the sunscreen and walk around like everybody else. A lot of those solutions became really fun because we got to play with those rules and mythologies. Ultimately, like *Supernatural* or any other show, you have to decide what your show is really about. Is it about a special effect or is it about the actors that you're paying a lot of money and that you're seeing every single week? For the people at home, it really does become about the actors and the metaphors behind these transformations.

Take a show like *Falling Skies*. There is some metaphor at work there, but really the plot demands that you deal with flesh-and-blood, nuts-and-bolts aliens. Those creatures aren't supernatural. They are really there. They have invaded our world, so that show quite wisely realized that it could not keep them in the shadows. We have to see the aliens and the Mechs, those big robot guys, walking around. They have to be a part of the world. That is a great part of that show, but you have to see them because they really exist. Thank God we do because that is what makes the show cool.

Fahy: What do you think are some of the biggest pitfalls in horror writing?

Hatem: For me, an overindulgence in surface-level trappings. When I look at the back of a book and it is about vampires that live on a different planet and have precognitive abilities, that is a problem. It's problem when you are staking thing on top of thing on top of thing. When a premise becomes too cluttered with rules and concepts then to me it is all icing and no cake. Now, certain people love that. For certain people, there can't be enough invention, but with me, I am a Stephen King guy. I'd rather have a 99.9 percent world that I recognize with one thing off.

Stephen King has a new book coming out next month called *Doctor Sleep*. This is a sequel to *The Shining*, so already you know you're in trouble. *The Shining* was all metaphor. *The Shining* was about a haunted house and the effect it has on people stuck in the house. Great! Haunted house. That is enough for a 500-page novel that millions of people around the world love. In the sequel, the little boy, Danny Torrance, has grown up, and he now works in a hospital as a hospice worker. Apparently, he is using his shining ability to know when people are about to die and to help them make that transition. That is one part of the story. Again, I have not read the book since it isn't out yet, but the second part of the book is about these other weird people—some sort of emotional vampires—traveling America. They are supernatural creatures that exist on whatever is exuded from a psychic when they are having a psychic experience. So they hunt down people like Danny, and they suck out their life force. At this point, I'm thinking: "I don't know what the fuck you're talking about." Again, my description is based on the paragraph you find on Amazon. I am willing to give Stephen King the benefit of the doubt. I will buy that book day one, and I will read it. And it might be brilliant. But I'm already worried because as a reader I don't need concept on top of concept. I don't need a world where there are vampires and other supernatural creatures that eat vampires. In those situations, I just don't know where the fuck I am. I'm not a vampire, and I'm not a vampire eater so why does this concern me.

Fahy: What is the best criticism that you have ever received as a writer?

Hatem: Well, that is a tricky question. Criticism can be either critical, or it can be: what is the best advice you ever got by way of criticism. I'll tell you what it is. It didn't make sense to me the first time I heard it, but it made sense as my career has progressed. Ironically enough, it is from Stephen King himself. This is something that he said either in *On Writing* or in some other interview. You know there is this famous story about King that he got halfway through the first draft of *Carrie* and threw it in the garbage. He felt that he wasn't interested in the story anymore. I'm bored. I don't think this is working. So he threw it away, and someone else picked it up and told him that it was working. What King learned from that and other similar experiences—and what I have found to be true—is that sometimes as a writer you're really, really interested in something that no one else gives a shit about. This is not to discount the enormous importance of personal passion when you write, but sometimes you have to step back. Sometimes, you have to look at your work for a long time from the vantage point of not being super interested on a gut level and recognize that this is the sort of story that should make sense, that usually does work. Then you have to keep at something until it finally takes flight down the line. The fact of the matter is you never know what people are going to love. I have written things that I thought were garbage that were produced and that people told me were their favorite things ever. I love it, love it, love it. The only response that you can possibly have to that is: "Thank you. I'm glad you loved it." (laughs) What you *don't* say is: "You loved that piece of shit? You're an idiot!" That would be the wrong answer.

Sometimes, you have to trust your inner voice, but every once in a while, trust an outer voice that tells you to keep going. There really is something here. Then work on faith and hope it all comes out in the end.

Grimm, Buffy the Vampire Slayer, and Angel

AN INTERVIEW WITH DAVID GREENWALT

After graduating from college, David Greewalt spent some time living in a trailer behind a friend's house and taking odd jobs. It wasn't until he found work as a movie extra that he decided to pursue a career in film and television. He wrote for a variety of shows, including *The X-Files*, before working with Joss Whedon on *Buffy the Vampire Slayer*. That show inspired him to co-create *Angel*. Currently, he is producing and writing *Grimm*, which he created along with Stephen Carpenter and Jim Kouf.

Fahy: I wanted to begin by asking you about fairy tales—

Greenwalt: Let me back up a moment. I don't consider what I have done to be horror TV although I consider it to be genre or maybe even fantasy TV. Although we do horrific things and it's a lot of fun to do an horrific thing, fairy tales provide another area where you have myth and some supernatural element, but you also have very grounded emotional dilemmas to deal with. So you have these very human emotions in a slightly, or sometimes more than slightly, supernatural world. It was my partner Jim Kouf who thought of the idea that our hero in *Grimm* would be able to see the monster within certain humans who are monstrous.

Of course, producers Todd Milliner (who sold *Grimm*) and Sean Hayes originally had the germ for this show. Todd told me, "There are 200 Grimm fairy tales. You've got ten years of shows here!" Of course, if you look at the Grimm fairy tales, there are only about

Monroe (Silas Weir Mitchell) reveals his inner identity as a Blutbad—a creature similar to a "Big Bad Wolf"—on *Grimm* (NBC). "Let Your Hair Down" (Season 1, Episode 7). NBC/Photofest, © NBC.

nine to eleven famous, well-known ones. The rest are obscure and really bizarre—like a talking donkey and a sausage go to town. (laughs)

We devised the notion that the people who wrote these fairy tales were in fact profilers. So what they wrote was true, and they were more than just cautionary tales. We also have the conceit that anyone who wrote fairy tales anywhere in the world had this ability. So in *Grimm* we draw on Japanese, Russian, African, Native American, and other myths. We were just looking at an Inuit myth this very morning. So we draw from a wide range of sources. One of the points of our show is to explain strange happenings. How do you explain a child molester? The Big Bad Wolf. How do you explain exorcism? Well, it has to do with what we call Wesen, which are the creatures within the humans.

Fahy: In some ways *Grimm* seems like the anti-Disney spin on these fairy tales. As a writer, when you're working with a fairy tale like "Sleeping Beauty," how conscious are you of writing against or playing with the Disney version that audiences are so accustomed to?

Greenwalt: It's not so much playing with it. Our vision is obviously a lot darker, but some of these fairy tales are quite gruesome. They're cutting off people's hands and feet. They're plucking out their eyes. We just want to take a little element of that and twist it. We did an episode that told the story of Cinderella one year later after she has been happily married to her Prince Charming. We took it from a different point of view.

We did do a big "Sleeping Beauty" arc in the second season with the character of Juliette, who fell into the coma and only some royal personage could awaken her. Instead of being a happy thing, that unleashed a very terrible thing in that they became madly attracted to each other and were fraught with guilt and passion.

Fahy: This is the problem if the wrong prince kisses you.
Greenwalt: (laughs) That's very good. I like that.

Fahy: You mentioned a few moments ago that many of the Grimm fairy tales were cautionary tales. They were designed, in part, to teach a moral lesson to children. When you think about the characters on the show, what are some of the lessons/morals that they are most in need of learning—other than don't sleep with a hexenbiest?
Greenwalt: Most of the characters are struggling with something. After Hank (Russell Hornsby) sees his first monster, for example, he considers giving up his job as a detective because he thinks he's going crazy. Aunt Marie tries to tell Nick about the Wesen and the legacy of his family, but he doesn't want to accept it at first. Rosalee has a substance abuse problem. Monroe, who is a Blutbad, which means "bloodbath" in German, has struggled to overcome his hunger for human flesh. And Juliette is having all sorts of troubles. Poor Juliette. (laughs)

For most of the characters, there are parts of the world and aspects of life that are difficult, nearly impossible, to comprehend, and these characters are struggling to confront those difficulties. There is something of value in that struggle.

Fahy: Those struggles make me think of that purification "milkshake" that Nick drinks in the second season. He still suffered when he drank it, which suggests that he is not pure of heart. What does he need to learn to develop as a character?

Greenwalt: Well, if you're looking for purity in a person, I think you'd need to find a baby to give that drink to. As human beings, we've all made bad choices and morally questionable decisions. There are many instances where Nick responds to a situation as a Grimm instead of a cop, and he sweeps some of those acts under the rug. So he is certainly not pure of heart. But he suffers less than Captain Renard, who is like a force of nature in that he starts off seeming to be evil and then seems to be good. He is caught somewhere between good and evil. But Nick is the hero. He is the moral center of the show.

Fahy: Even with all of your experience, I would imagine that seeing actors bring alive your writing must still be a thrill. Have there been any performances by the actors in *Grimm* that surprised you, that made you develop a character in a different way?

Greenwalt: We really have an embarrassment of talent on this show—such a gifted cast and crew. They are all great. I think Monroe (Silas Weir Mitchell) is one of the standout characters. He is someone who has wrestled with his urges and seems to have them under control. He likes Pilates, classical music, fine wine, and gourmet food. You also suspect that he takes some kind of medication to control his urges, but in general, he is a character who has overcome his dangerous hungers, his inner demons. In many ways, he is the character who is easiest for me and Jim to write.

It's also funny that Silas is so similar to his character. They both posses a great deal of knowledge, go off on tangents, and know a lot about wine. The actor least like his character is Sasha Roiz. Sasha is so funny and self-deprecating. He is completely different from Captain Renard.

But to get back to your question, Adalind Schade (Claire Coffee) originally had only a small role in the pilot, but she was so deliciously evil that we had to bring her and the figure of the hexenbiest back. Now she is a regular on the show.

Fahy: Hexenbiests seem to be running amok in *Grimm*. Witchcraft and magic are an integral part of the show—as they were in *Buffy the Vampire Slayer*, *Angel*, and at times on *The X-Files*. After so many years of delving into the supernatural as a writer, do you believe in any supernatural phenomenon?

Greenwalt: It's funny you ask that. I remember working on *The X-Files*. I didn't work on the show for long, but it was very intense work for a couple of months. At one point, I remember wondering if I might actually see an alien. (laughs)

Fahy: You seemed to reference that in *Grimm* with the Wesen that has blue-glowing skin and looks like an alien.

Greenwalt: Yes, the blue glowing man (Glühenvolk) that was killing cattle. In that episode, we also had Sergeant Wu say, "The truth is out there." Another nod to *The X-Files*.

But to answer your question, no. I don't believe in supernatural phenomenon. So if you were to ask me if I believe in witches, I don't think they exist, but I don't know for sure. This doesn't mean that the supernatural can't be real for some people. If someone believes in something, it can have a powerful impact on them psychologically. The mind is a powerful thing.

I do believe we live in a world where many things are difficult to explain and to comprehend. Science often makes us think that the world can be broken down into tens of millions of particles. But to quote Shakespeare, "There are more things in heaven and earth, than are dreamt of in your philosophy." I recently read that most of the universe is comprised of black holes and dark matter, which seems to be a reminder of how much about the world and universe we don't really understand.

For me, the supernatural is a wonderful metaphor for trying to come to terms with the things we can't explain in the world around us. That is what makes the supernatural so great to work with as a writer.

Fahy: As I just mentioned, you spent many years as a writer and producer on *Buffy the Vampire Slayer*, which also grew into another show that you co-created, *Angel*. Since these shows, vampires have become fairly common on television and film. What is it about vampires that you think make them so popular today? Why are we so drawn to that mythology?

Greenwalt: It's funny because after I worked on *Angel* I thought that would be the last word on television vampires, and now I can't believe how many vampire shows there are! (laughs) I think it is the bad-boy aspect of vampires that make them so popular—being drawn to something dangerous and unpredictable.

Joss Whedon's concept for *Buffy* was so great. Here was this blonde teenage girl who ran down dark alleys and beat the shit out of monsters. Her attraction to Angel was also an attraction to the dangerous bad boy. One of the great moments of the show involved a curse that had been put on Angel. If he ever experienced a moment of true happiness, he would lose his soul and become a complete cad. Of course, this moment happens when he sleeps with Buffy. I've spoken to many women about this show, women of all ages—from college girls to forty-year-old mothers—and they can all relate to that storyline.

Fahy: What was it about the character Angel that inspired you to co-create a show about his adventures?

Greenwalt: Angel is really the oldest twenty-eight-year-old in history. He had been alive for centuries, so he had all of this experience, knowledge, heartache, guilt, and remorse. That made him a really interesting character to write. In *Buffy*, we were dealing with characters that were coming-of-age, and coming-of-age is a wonderful theme to deal with. The teenage years can be some of the most transformative in a person's life—more so than the twenties, in my opinion—and the supernatural element of the show added a rich dimension to exploring teenage angst. We had one episode in *Buffy the Vampire Slayer*, for example, in which a girl felt so insignificant, so inconsequential that she literally became invisible ("Out of Mind, Out of Sight"). I think most people can remember feeling that way back in high school.

Our original idea for *Angel* was to make a private-eye show in the style of Mike Hammer. We were featuring a lone hero in a big city who was willing to use violence to get justice. We also intended to make the show much darker than *Buffy*. In an early episode, we had a scene in which Angel drank the blood of a victim he couldn't save, and the network was horrified. They thought that it was too dark and that we had gone too far. They were right. We hadn't prepared the audience for that. So we lightened the tone.

In addition to having David Boreanaz, we also brought with us the fantastic Charisma Carpenter, and her character (Cordelia) provided the right kind of humorous balance and wit to the show.

"THE SIMPLEST STORIES PRODUCE THE RICHEST CHARACTERS."

—DAVID GREENWALT

Fahy: I remember this wonderful episode in *Buffy the Vampire Slayer* where Buffy can read minds. This ability becomes overwhelming, especially as she discovers that everyone is thinking something completely different from what they are saying. But when Buffy "hears" Cordelia's thoughts, there is no filter whatsoever. She says exactly what she is thinking.

Greenwalt: (laughs) Exactly. That kind of humor, which Joss is so great at, is something that we wanted for *Angel*.

Fahy: When you look back at your work on *Buffy the Vampire Slayer* and *Angel*, how did those shows impact your approach to *Grimm*?
Greenwalt: Before writing for those shows, I wrote films and other shows like *Profit* and *The Wonder Years*. I wouldn't call myself a horror writer. As I mentioned earlier, we certainly have a lot of gruesome things on *Grimm*, but I never think of myself in those terms. Ultimately, it's about creating characters that resonate with audiences and telling good stories. So I think we could achieve similar things if we were writing a Western. But—I know I'm repeating myself here—it was Joss Whedon who introduced me to the supernatural. A lot of the writers on *Buffy* read comic books throughout their lives, but that wasn't the case for me. It was through my work on *Buffy* that I could see the rich possibilities the supernatural offered for storytelling. It can make struggles and triumphs of a character even more dramatic, more intense.

Fahy: To shift focus to more writerly questions, when did you know you wanted to be a writer?
Greenwalt: I knew I wanted to be a writer when I was a child. Then I went to college at the University of Redlands. I wasn't an English major. I was doing some kind of English-Education degree. But after I started taking English classes, I realized, "Wow, this is really hard." After college, I wandered around for a while. I did odd jobs—working as a waiter, a bartender. I lived in a trailer on a friend's property in Malibu, so I was basically living for free. Then in my mid-twenties, I did some work as an extra on a movie. It was an eye-opening experience. It completely demystified the process of movie making for me. I realized that someone wrote the script. Some people read the lines. Some director—whether he understood the script or not—shot it.

So in my mid twenties, I started writing screenplays. Jim went on to a very successful film career. He wrote big films like *Stakeout*, *Rush Hour*, and *National Treasure*. But I gravitated toward television. I love television writing. It's a place where the writer is important—as it should be. I also like the immediacy of television. A film can take several years to produce, and it can die on a Friday night. Like lots of screenwriters, I dream of writing a novel or a musical one day. But I'm busy with this work right now, and I love it. I'm happy to be working. Times are tough out there.

Fahy: What are some of your other early influences that had an impact on your writing? And what do you consider to be one of your favorite horror works?

Greenwalt: William Goldman. I was definitely influenced by William Goldman's *Butch Cassidy and the Sundance Kid.* If you haven't read the script, you should. Though it's not formatted like a typical screenplay, it reads so well. It's published in book form, and it reads like a great novel or short story. *The Godfather* is another masterpiece that had a big impact on me.

I also remember watching *Bret Maverick* with James Garner. If you watch it now, the production value isn't very good, but that's not how I remember it. Garner could save the girl or not save the girl. He was a reluctant hero. I'm drawn to that figure of the reluctant hero.

Fahy: Horror fans seem to crave both novelty and the familiar. How do you keep it fresh as a writer?

Greenwalt: I've now been to Comic Con three times, and I've met the rabid fans there. They are wonderful and so dedicated. They also care about writers—not just the stars—and that is very flattering for those of us behind the scenes.

It is always a challenge keeping it fresh. Writing is very different from other professions. Let's say you were a heart surgeon who performs bypass surgeries. One day, you perform a surgery, and then next day you perform the same surgery. So your skills improve by doing the same thing over and over again—assuming that medical thinking about that kind of heart surgery stays the same. With writing, it doesn't really work that way. Yes, I know a lot of tricks. I know what I've done before, how I've handled certain situations. But it still has to be new every time. So every day, you're faced with the blank page. And every day, you wonder why you chose this profession. (laughs)

One of the things I like to do is to confront a character with a situation that turns his/her world upside down. Take *The Bridge on the River Kwai*, for example. Shears (William Holden) escapes from prison, but midway through the film, he is asked to return to the prison and destroy the bridge. At that moment, his world gets turned upside down. He is horrified by the prospect of going back. We try to do that in *Grimm*. At the midpoint of an episode, we try to confront a character with something that turns his world upside down for a moment, and then he has to deal.

Fahy: What do you think are some of the biggest pitfalls in horror writing?

Greenwalt: Again, I think it comes down to the characters. They need to be three-dimensional. I would say the biggest pitfall is writing one-dimensional characters. Don't make the bad guys all bad. They have to be struggling. Maybe the villain hurt someone to protect his own family. Maybe there is something else about him that mitigates some of his actions. Those are the types of villains we like to write for *Grimm*. Of course, we recently had a creature named Volcanalis, who was a mythical fire demon. He was this destructive force of nature, and he was pretty scary. But in general, we try to write multidimensional bad guys with complex motivations and layers. It gives you and the audience more places to go.

I've heard people pitch ideas where they want to write a story with all of these complicated twists and turns, but at some point, the characters get lost. For me, it's about characters. The audience needs to have an emotional connection with the characters. We need to be invested in what happens to them. I think the simplest stories produce the richest characters.

Fahy: What was the best criticism you ever received?
Greenwalt: Cut this. (laughs)
    I would say the best criticism I ever received was to revise.

Fahy: I tell my students that all the time.
Greenwalt: Revision, revision, revision. It is the most important thing to producing good writing. Rewriting is so crucial. Jim and I are often faced with a script that needs to be cut, and that process involves thinking about each word. What is the right word here? What is essential for this scene, for this character? When you are revising, you focus on each detail to achieve . . .

Fahy: An economy of language?
Greenwalt: Yes, an economy of language. You only achieve that by rewriting things. That doesn't mean that you don't have freedom to explore ideas. When Jim writes, he is very focused, and I've learned a lot from that. He also knows how to let a story go in directions where it can still surprise you. I tend to want a roadmap, but working with Jim has helped me open up to those surprises that make the genre so great.

Fahy: Does your own work ever scare you when you finally see it on screen?
Greenwalt: It still makes me laugh. We sometimes have these *Grimm* parties with thirty or so people, and a lot of them get scared, which is great. My girlfriend jumps at the scary parts. So that is rewarding. But for me, the humor always works.

Fahy: In addition to writing, you've also directed several episodes in *Angel.* Would you like to do more directing?
Greenwalt: I also directed episodes of *Buffy* and *The Wonder Years.*

I think for a lot of writers directing is a great way to capture the nuances of your story, to get exactly what you want. But to tell you the truth, it is a hell of a lot of work. It demands so much time, and if I were to get back into that, I'd really need to get in shape. And I really hate the idea of getting in shape. (laughs)

Besides, we have so many wonderful directors on the show that I don't think to myself that I really need to do that. I would like to direct an episode with Jim, but I don't want to invest the time into directing. I'm sixty-two. I have a great schedule right now, and I'd like to keep that.

The Walking Dead

Gale Anne Hurd co-wrote and produced *The Terminator* in 1984, and ever since she has produced some of the most popular, engaging, and terrifying works of horror and science fiction—including *Aliens* (1986), *The Abyss* (1989), *Tremors* (1990), *Terminator 2: Judgment Day* (1991), *The Relic* (1997), and *Hulk* (2003). In 2010, she began producing the AMC series *The Walking Dead*.

Fahy: I'd like to start on a playful note, if you don't mind. I'm fascinated by the zombies on *The Walking Dead*. They seem to be on camera a lot, so they must not have much time for careers outside of being on the show. Who are all of those extras?

Hurd: A lot of them are professional extras out of the Atlanta area. We have our go-to people. It is actually an incredibly demanding and difficult job in incredibly brutal conditions. So a lot of them are professional extras. A lot of them don't just play zombies or as we call them "Walkers." Some people have auditioned on our zombie school day. They do it for fun and take vacation days from their jobs.

Fahy: I've seen some footage of your zombie school, and it does seem like being a zombie is hard work.

Hurd: It is. It's incredibly hard work. You know, some people can't make it through the day because of heat exhaustion. Some people don't respond well to the makeup or humidity. On top of that, we've got ticks, chiggers, and mosquitoes.

Fahy: More seriously, Greg Nicotero is your wonderful special effects makeup artist on *The Walking Dead*, which some would say is a dying art. Do you find makeup more effective than CGI? Does it add a quality to *The Walking Dead* that you wouldn't get otherwise?

Hurd: Well, I actually think it is not a dying art. If you are creating an entire character where you can't put makeup on an entire person, then, yes, you do need to resort to CGI. But I actually find more and more makeup artists working—especially doing prosthetic makeup. In fact, I am a guest judge from time to time on this show on Syfy called *Face-Off* where they're looking to find the next great prosthetics makeup artist. There is so much that goes into it. You have to design the makeup. You have to create it depending on the conditions. You have to modify it especially when you're shooting in heat and humidity. You also have to have prosthetics that work in cold weather or in dry weather. So it is really a complicated art.

Fahy: Do you feel your reliance on makeup art has added a richer dimension to *The Walking Dead*?

Hurd: One would never approach it through CGI. I know that *World War Z* did, but I think CGI never feels real. We want to be up-close. We want to be right in there with our characters because our series is very character-driven, and the jeopardy they're in is up-close and personal. You can achieve that through makeup because you have *two* performers working. You have the person who is portraying the Walker as well as the actor from the show. So you can give them direction. You can create a lot more nuance. And you get it in camera, so you know exactly what it's going to look like. You actually have the actor interacting with someone as opposed to with nothing. So they can perform it like any other scene. That makes a *huge* difference.

Fahy: This makes me think of another aspect of the show—the audience. I think it is fair to say that certain types of horror works speak to different audiences in terms of gender. Vampire stories are

It isn't easy being a zombie—or anyone else for that matter—on *The Walking Dead* (AMC). "Days Gone Bye" (Season 1, Episode 1). © AMC.

often geared toward women by emphasizing romance and featuring seductive male vampires, whereas zombie stories have typically appealed to male audiences. Yet *The Walking Dead* has been able to draw large numbers of both men and women. What is it about *The Walking Dead* that is working for women, that is drawing them to the show?

Hurd: Well, I think that the surprising thing is that the horror genre has always drawn a lot of women. Always. If you look at the demographics of horror films and even of what one would call "slasher films," teen girls are some of the largest demographics. They are the ones who actually drive the cinema-going. What is more surprising to me, actually, is that horror and *The Walking Dead* appeal to people that are older than teens. For our show, I think it comes from the fact that it is character-driven. You fall in love with the characters.

What I also find surprising is the number of people who say, "I never thought I would have watched a show like this. I watched the first episode, and I've stayed with it ever since." I do think this happens because of the show's characters. As an audience, we can identify with them and the moral choices they have to make.

Fahy: So the appeal of the show boils down to the connection the audience—women as well as men—have with the characters.

Hurd: Yes, we have a strong ensemble cast. People identify with certain cast members, and I believe our most vocal fans are the female fans. If you look on Twitter and often on Facebook, they are the ones who are driving the conversation.

Fahy: There was certainly a lot of debate last season over Andrea's character and her choices, and many of those online debater were happening among female viewers.

Hurd: Yes. Absolutely.

Fahy: Do you feel that you bring a different perspective to the show as a woman? It seems that most of the writers and producers are men. Do you sometimes find yourself offering a viewpoint that is slightly different?

Hurd: You know, I think we are all very much on the same page. If you go back to Robert Kirkman's comic books, our underlying source material, the women in his comic books are fantastic. I don't think you necessarily have to be female in order to write or create strong women characters. We actually have three women in our writers' room this season. And we have a significant number of women directors as well.

Fahy: Once you're in production, how do you achieve the balance between staying on schedule and budget without compromising the creativity of the project? That must be difficult at times.

Hurd: It is. Television is far more difficult than features. You start another episode every eight days. You can't go over. Otherwise, the train really goes off the tracks. But we have such a fantastic cast and crew. They are up for it. There are no weak links. For directors who are new to the show, it tends to be a shock to the system even though we say to them that this may be the hardest show they have ever done. You don't really realize it until you're there in the elements with 150 Walker extras, and you simply can't go over [that filming period]. We are also lucky because in our arsenal Greg Nicotero, whom you mentioned before, is also our second unit director in addition to directing a number of episodes himself. He directed the season premiere this year ("30 Days Without an Accident") for season four. So we can pick up a few things if we drop them.

Fahy: In terms of the content itself, when you're dealing with gruesome, horrific material, is there a line you won't cross as a filmmaker? Have you ever cut scenes from your own work that you ultimately thought went too far, were too scary?

Hurd: The way we look at it on *The Walking Dead* is that we don't do things for gratuitous ends. It is all about bringing our characters to life and servicing their story. When the character of Rick essentially went crazy in season three, he became a lot more brutal. And you have to show that. You are also able to see the differences among characters by showing how they respond to horrible things. One of the things that elucidated Shane's character was the moment he shot Otis and left him behind essentially to be zombie food so that he could escape and save Carl's life ("Save the Last One"). That is not something that Rick Grimes would have done.

Obviously, there are some things that are a lot of fun, like the well zombie ("Cherokee Rose"). We also made sure that when we pulled the well zombie up and he split in half that you got to see the cast's reaction to that. Even IronE Singleton, who played T-Dog, almost threw up himself just watching it. (laughs) Once again, it's not only showing moments like that; it's showing our characters' reaction.

Fahy: You have an impressive and extensive career as a film producer. What were some of your early influences—particularly in horror and science fiction—that inspired your work?

Hurd: Going way, way back with fantasy and science fiction, I loved Ray Bradbury, Clifford Simak, Arthur C. Clarke, Philip K.

Dick, Frank Herbert, Roger Zelazny, Clive Barker, and, of course, Stephen King. I was also influenced by George Romero's work in film. What I love is that now this work is given the recognition that it has long deserved. It is no longer considered in the exploitation subgenre.

I started reading comic books when I was about four, and then I became a huge science fiction, fantasy, and horror fan when I started reading books. I was a voracious reader. I read between ten and fourteen books a week. I did not have much of a social life. (laughs)

Fahy: You were a voracious reader, and you went on to co-write your first major film, *The Terminator*. What moved you in the direction of production as opposed to focusing more on writing?

Hurd: I like to be around people. I like to be part of a collaboration. I don't think I knew at the time that there was a possibility of joining a writing staff on a TV series. And TV, of course, is very much a collaborative medium. I just wasn't cut out for sitting at home by myself. Back then it would have been in front of an IBM Selectric typewriter. So production was perfect for me because it was collaborative. You are sharing your vision with the director and the writers. It really is that triumvirate. And you also get to make sure that the cast and crew are all on the same page.

Fahy: You have certainly spent a lot of time thinking about this genre, so I'm curious as to what you consider some of the biggest pitfalls in horror writing?

Hurd: I think the greatest pitfall, regardless of genre, is not having the characters be at the center of your story. If you focus primarily on the plot and try to shoehorn the characters in later, that just doesn't work. So I think that everything has to evolve from character regardless of genre. If you really don't feel for a character who is in jeopardy, then you have lost the audience. And you have lost me as well.

Hemlock Grove

AN INTERVIEW WITH BRIAN McGREEVY

Brian McGreevy earned his MFA in creative writing at the University of Texas at Austin. He realized he was onto something good when his thesis advisor told him to throw away the manuscript for *Hemlock Grove*. Instead of taking that advice, he got a book deal with Farrar, Straus and Giroux and then adapted it into a miniseries for Netflix, with Eli Roth directing the first episode.

Fahy: Let's talk about werewolves. Why werewolves? What is it about the werewolf legend that inspired you to explore it in your first novel?

McGreevy: I have a theory on that. The term "therianthropy" describes the very common mythological motif of humans turning into animals. Far and away the most common subgenre of this motif is lycanthropy—people turning into wolves—and this is something that exists in almost every major cultural system in history. I believe that the reason for that is that human beings and dogs coevolved. X-number of generations ago all dogs were wolves, but as they became increasingly dependent on humans for their survival, and as a result became substantially less strong and intelligent than wolves, the canine that exists today came into being. As a result of that, when we are relating ourselves to our own animal pasts and animal nature, the easiest link that we find relatable is on the canine side.

Fahy: So in one way, you're saying that it is about going back and trying to think more about our origins—particularly as they are related to what is animalistic about all of us.

McGreevy: Yes, that is correct. I would say that in every human being there is a necessary tension between the neocortex and the limbic system. The werewolf is just a means for us to do this.

Fahy: Early in the novel, Roman witnesses Peter's transformation into a wolf, and he describes the experience as a privilege. Can you talk a little bit more about the way you use the werewolf as a metaphor for change?

McGreevy: So the transformation in the book was the most direct metaphor for childbirth, which is a process that is very violent and very gruesome in its way, but it is also a highly organic part of the life cycle. It's also an example of the extreme degree of physical metamorphosis the human body undergoes. When you look at a newborn baby and an elderly adult and consider that that is the same organism, it is really remarkable that as a human you really do go through several incarnations through your lifetime. Consider how protean and elastic the female body is; it is a vehicle for generating and gestating life. I wanted to take something that was conventionally horrific and try to find something majestic about it.

Fahy: You also include the myth of the *upir*—a vampire in Eastern European culture that can live in the daylight, eats children, and doesn't believe in God. Roman—one of the main characters—longs to be a warrior of sorts, but did he ever really stand a chance? Was he ever going to break free from his "inheritance" as an *upir*?

McGreevy: I would say that he probably is going to be a warrior but on the profoundly wrong side.

Fahy: He is not going to transcend his nature.

McGreevy: In theory he could have transcended it, but fate—and by fate I mean the author—took away every possible source of support that could give him that strength (i.e., Letha, Shelley, and Peter).

Fahy: So without a community there is no way for him to overcome his nature.

McGreevy: Ostensibly, if any of the three of them were ultimately around, [things had the potential to be different]. Roman does have a good heart. I think that by in large I fall somewhere between the nature and nurture argument. Nature, I do believe, obviously plays a significant role, but if you take someone who becomes a sadistic, destructive immoral person, the right environmental change (and by the right environmental change I mean fundamentally being surrounded by love or feeling love) could drastically change the path of the person.

"SO THE NUTSHELL IDEA OF [*HEMLOCK GROVE*] WAS TO TAKE DRACULA, FRANKENSTEIN, AND THE WOLFMAN AND PUT THEM IN MY HIGH SCHOOL."

—BRIAN McGREEVY

Fahy: You know, there were moments in the televised adaptation where Roman's hypnotic stare reminded me of the wonderful Bela Lugosi in Tod Browning's *Dracula*. Were those early horror films an influence for you as a writer and filmmaker?

McGreevy: The Browning version of *Dracula* was hugely influential on me—much more so than the source novel, which I didn't read until after I had written a draft of *Hemlock Grove*. And then I thought I should read it for its context. I pretty much wanted to be working with the iconography of the genre and the iconography of the genre cinematically much more so than from a literary perspective. If I'm being honest, I'm not particularly well read in the horror genre of books, but I have seen very, very, very many horror movies. There was something about the canonical monster movies that Universal was making in that period that was very striking to me. One of the main inspirations of the book was being in a video store in Austin, Texas, when I was in graduate school, and these beautiful new editions of those movies came out with these gleaming, platinum covers. I just knew from a mythopoeic perspective that I found them endlessly fascinating. At one point, the title for the novel was "Universal Monsters."

So the nutshell idea of the book was to take Dracula, Frankenstein, and the Wolfman and put them in my high school. (laughs)

Fahy: They're all well represented there.

McGreevy: Yeah. But take, for instance, one of the earliest choices in writing the book. It was to avoid the term "vampire" completely. That word is never used in the book, which is really just a pretty transparent sleight of hand because "upir" itself is a Slavic synonym for the word vampire. But I knew that there was this cultural freight that came along with the word [vampire] and that there was this very legalistic interpretation of the archetype like "these are the rules." But the rules were not actually based on folklore or existing literature really. They were based on rules that had been made by movies. For instance, in the novel *Dracula*, his powers are actually quite nebulously defined, and he walks around in the daylight all the time. I knew that if I was going to be working with these tropes—like the Frankenstein character, the Dracula character, et cetera—that there was some onus on me to take what was conventionally thought about them through a pop-cultural lens and discard everything that I found un-useful to create the sense of mystery that I think makes this genre so strangely appealing.

Fahy: This topic anticipates my next question. I was just about to ask how you deal with the challenges of taking these conventional mythologies and trying to keep them fresh as a writer, which you just addressed. It makes me think that one of the striking things about *Hemlock Grove* is that werewolves are not monsters. The

One of the iconic "Universal" monsters played by Boris Karloff (*Frankenstein*, 1931). Directed by James Whale.
Photographers: Jack Freulich, Sherman Clark. Universal Pictures/Photofest, © Universal Pictures.

character Christina is a monster, but she goes outside the natural order of things and becomes a *vargulf*, which Peter explains is "'a wolf that's gone insane. . . . [It] doesn't eat what it kills.'" But werewolfism is described as beautiful and as part of the natural world. That seems to me to be one area which you were trying not to fall into old patters and, as you said, to reject some of those old rules.

McGreevy: That goes along with a theory I have about adolescence and psychosexual development. If I saw a seventeen-year-old young man who was too orderly and liked going to school and liked obeying rules, it would hurt my heart because I want to see them drink too much beer and set some shit on fire and be highly unruly. (laughs)

And I don't think those activities in any way necessarily exclusive to having a good heart and being a sensitive, conscientious person. My feeling with Peter is that, pound for pound, he is probably the wisest character in the book. Or he might be in competition with Olivia for that, but Olivia is also someone who is completely comfortable with her own nature.

Fahy: Yes, that wisdom comes from a very different place. In the process of adapting the book, you must have seen opportunities to explore some elements of the material differently. What were some aspects of the book that you were most interested in developing as you wrote the teleplays?

McGreevy: Writing a novel and producing any kind of cinematic adaptation—let alone a cinematic adaptation of that length—are very different experiences. One is a very solitary process, and the other is a very non-solitary process. So I would say that the adaptation largely consisted of what material other voices in the process wanted to see expanded.

Fahy: There is great deal of additional material about Dr. Chasseur, for example. So that came from the collaborative process of making the series?

McGreevy: A number of things that made it into the series had been incorporated into earlier drafts of the book, but were excised before the draft that was published because I found that the further things were being taken from the core narrative of Peter and Roman the more I was doing the reader a disservice. This kind of novel has an ensemble element but much less so than a TV series. So a lot of Chasseur's backstory, motivation, and patterns of self destruction did emerge in the show from discarded material from the novel.

Fahy: The adaptation certainly remains very faithful to the book. How influential was Eli Roth in establishing the "look" of the show?
McGreevy: It's pretty much his stamp as a director of the first episode.

Fahy: How did your collaboration with him come about? How did he first get interested in *Hemlock Grove*?
McGreevy: I had sold the book to Farrar Straus, but it wasn't coming out for another year. I took it around town and met with producers. Because I had been working in that industry for a couple of years as a screenwriter, I was familiar with the landscape. I met with a number of producers, and I met with them with two criteria. One criterion was that I was going to be an executive producer on the project. The other was that this was going to be a hard "R" because there wasn't really any purpose of doing it if we were going to do the *Twilight* version of it. That was how I started working with Eric Newman who is an executive producer on the project and Eli Roth's producing partner. Eric was the one who took it to Eli.

Fahy: What do you think about producing your show through Netflix? Netflix has had tremendous success with its original programming. What were some the benefits of doing this with Netflix?
McGreevy: Netflix was our goal all along. At roughly the time we all came together on the producer end, the *House of Cards* deal was announced. None of us were TV guys. None of us had much

investment in the conventional wisdom in that industry. When we saw what Netflix was willing to commit to upfront, we looked at each other and thought: "Fuck, we want that!" (laughs)

We had a couple of offers from more predictable cable outlets that in and of themselves would have been a fine home for this, but they just weren't offering what Netflix was.

Fahy: I'd like to come back to some writerly questions. When did you know you wanted to be a writer and a horror writer more specifically?

McGreevy: I've known I wanted to be a writer pretty much my entire life. It goes back to something I wrote for a class when I was seven years old and is still in a box of memorabilia underneath my mother's bed.

To be perfectly honest, I don't consider myself a horror writer. *Hemlock Grove* as a novel was a pretty conscious attempt to use the basic structure and tropes of the gothic novel as a lens to examine my own adolescence. For instance, the house that published it, Farrar Straus, is not a genre publisher, and frankly it isn't even an especially commercial publisher. To me, it was a highly subjective experiment that just so happened to strike a chord with audiences.

Fahy: We've talked about the influence of those Universal horror films in the 1930s on your work. What were some other early influences in film and writing?

McGreevy: On the film side, at a pretty young age, I was obsessed with Alfred Hitchcock. There were things he was doing that struck me even in preadolescence that I didn't have a vocabulary for, but I had an intuitive sense that I was interested in that. For example, the employment of an odd or unconventional camera angle for a given scene, possibly even a mundane scene, that creates a sense of tension and dread. The formal dramatic term for that is the "alienation effect," which is intentionally making a stylistic choice that drives the audience out. When they are driven out, they engage with the scene in a different way. When I was twelve, I wasn't thinking correctly in dramatic terms. I was studying his work—just curious about why it was having the impact on me that it was. Overall, he was probably my biggest cinematic influence.

As far as literary influences, there are probably too many to get into. I spent seven years of higher education studying writing and books.

Fahy: What do you think are some of the biggest pitfalls in horror writing?

McGreevy: I'm not sure that I know. For me, all I knew was that I was writing what was most interesting to me at the moment. I would say I have a fairly healthy and communicative relationship with my own unconscious and the darker recesses therein. Fucked-up and nightmarish imagery comes to me somewhat effortlessly. So tapping into that frankly wasn't that much of a challenge. (laughs) For me, it was just the serendipitous confluence of the fact that what I was most compelled to explore on the page happened to have market potential.

Fahy: What was the best criticism you ever received as a writer?

McGreevy: My thesis advisor—because I started writing this book in graduate school and it ultimately was my thesis—gave me the advice to throw it away. The reason I think that was some of the most valuable advice I ever got was because it taught me the value of ignoring advice. (laughs)

At the time I was twenty-three years old. I had just written a draft of a weird, little postmodern horror novel about my hometown, and someone who knew better and genuinely had my best interests at heart was saying, "Now throw this away and write a real book." It's not like I had any justification beyond sheer instinct to believe he was wrong, but I knew he was wrong.

Fahy: It seems like graduate school is often filled with moments like that.
McGreevy: Oh, yeah.

Fahy: What are you working on now?
McGreevy: I am currently working on a new, unrelated novel.

Fahy: So you plan to keep moving back and forth between film and novel writing?
McGreevy: Yes. I recently started a production company with my writing partner called Shinebox SMC. We produced *Hemlock Grove*, and we have a few other things in development right now that will probably go into production in the next year. So rather than going into academia, I ended up as a novelist with film and TV producing as my day job.

Fahy: That's not a bad alternative. I'm curious about something else, which takes us back to the production side of things for *Hemlock Grove*. Were the special effects complicated for this show?
McGreevy: They were, but I had so little involvement with the production side of things. What I knew about that stuff came more or less from headache-inducing conversations about budgets and sitting around and drinking with the actors. I know Landon [Liboiron] spent a lot of time semi-clothed in the mud. I really enjoyed putting actors through just as punishing situations as I put my characters through. I would say that I'm as destructive a force as a producer as I am an author.

Fahy: Then I look forward to reading your next novel, and I feel sorry for the actors who will have to take it on.
McGreevy: Oh, they should be so lucky. (laughs)

Being Human

AN INTERVIEW WITH ANNA FRICKE

Anna Fricke grew up in Maine near to a cemetery—a setting that inspired her interest in ghost stories as a child—so perhaps it is no surprise that she eventually found her way to writing horror. Prior to her work on the American adaptation of *Being Human*, she wrote for the series *Dawson's Creek*, *Touching Evil*, and *Everwood*. In 2014, she signed a deal with Twentieth Century Fox to become the showrunner for *Hieroglyph*.

Fahy: What about the British series *Being Human* inspired you to adapt it? Was there something about the story and characters that you were particularly interested in exploring as a writer?

Fricke: My husband, Jeremy Carver, who now runs *Supernatural,* and I started it together. The project was brought to us actually. We have the same agent, and he thought it might be interesting as something for us to partner on. We had never partnered on anything before; we had always written separately. Leading up to *Being Human*, Jeremy had been working on *Supernatural*, and I had been doing mostly character dramas like *Everwood* and *Dawson's Creek*. So in a way, we were both sides of the coin in terms of genre and character, and that is what *Being Human* is as a show. He and I don't see ourselves as fitting strictly in those boxes. I've always been a fan of genre, and he has always been a fan of character. We wanted to expand those interests a little bit for our careers, and *Being Human* was a way to do that. Also, in terms of the show, we really fell in love with the way it was a genre show in this sea of supernatural, horror shows that really was just a character drama at the heart of it.

We always felt that if you took away the special effects, if you took away the supernatural quality, the story should still work. It should still be about these people just struggling and trying to make it and having normal relationships. They definitely have big problems and issues, but they are people—somewhere down there beneath it all. So we liked that. And we liked that it was a rough and dark and funny and a little messy. All of that was appealing.

Fahy: As far as genre goes, *Being Human* packs almost every gothic convention into one nice, neat package . . . or house, in this case. Were you a fan of gothic horror—vampire stories, ghost stories, and such—before the show?

Fricke: I think more so when I was a kid, though I definitely keep up with vampire shows. I watch *True Blood* and *The Vampire Diaries.*

I grew up in Maine in the woods by a cemetery—all very Stephen King—so I think that growing up in that environment and being a latchkey child and having a wild imagination explains part of the appeal for me. I was always really drawn to ghost stories as a kid. I sort of grew up reading those books from that Time Warner series. Do you remember those? The series had something like twelve books. One book was about ghosts, another one was about witches. The series collected all of these great old stories—fables, ghost stories, and things like that from all around the world. I was obsessed with those books when I was little, and I think that interest had a lasting effect.

Also, my dad showed me *The Shining* when I was five, which I always thought was some sort of family joke. (laughs) But last year I asked him, "Dad, did you really show me *The Shining* when I was five?" He said, "Yeah!" He thought it was the greatest thing ever. He was really proud of the fact that he had. "Well, look at your career," he said. "I obviously influenced you, and you're doing fine."

Fahy: When you do tackle these myths now as a writer, what are your favorite aspects to play with?

Fricke: I had a healthy belief in ghosts as a kid, and I feel like the things that give you the chills when you're eleven or twelve years old are still the best things. The very basic scares are still the ones that get me. The more believable they are the better they are. If you think this could conceivably happen to you, that is the scariest thing. What I and the other writers try to do on the show is not to worry so much about what the rules are in every other show or movie like ours, but instead we focus on what makes sense. As long as the horror is grounded in something believable or really emotional, then that is where it lives. That is the most fun for me to play with: what can you relate back to yourself that will make this moment affect you more?

"I FEEL LIKE THE THINGS THAT GIVE YOU THE CHILLS WHEN YOU'RE ELEVEN OR TWELVE YEARS OLD ARE STILL THE BEST THINGS."

—ANNA FRICKE

Fahy: What makes monsters such good metaphors/vehicles for exploring human nature?
Fricke: I guess because you can do such fantastical things with them. A monster can reflect the best and worst parts of yourself. When you look at a vampire, they are super fast and they're super sexy and they're strong and they can't die, which is all really exciting as a kind of wish fulfillment. But we really like to play with the idea on the show that at the heart of it they are just drug addicts. They're just these suffering, psychopathic drug addicts. (laughs) I guess it is fun to play with because it takes whatever you might relate to in yourself—whether it be an addiction or an emotional crutch or loneliness—and turns up the volume on it. Seeing these issues through monsters makes it fun. You can see those figures

holding up a mirror to you, but you can also rise above whatever is going on in your life and escape it a little bit—because no one is ever going to be as bad or as crazy or as dangerous as a monster. So it is a fun way to detach yourself for a little while from whatever your problems are.

Fahy: You mention this issue of addiction, and Aiden is very much presented as a blood addict. Much of the show seems to be about issues fundamental to human nature (as the title would suggest)—addiction, transformation, being haunted by the past, desiring to be more than what we are. Are there certain themes that you are most interested in exploring as a writer on the show?

Fricke: Definitely. Every season we approach with a theme in mind: what is our journey for this year going to be? For season four, the focus is the past coming back to haunt them. In addition to themes, we play with a lot of other things like class issues. That seems to be a classic characteristic in the genre as a whole—exploring the class and racial undertones between vampires and werewolves. We've also looked into domestic violence with Sally's character. And a lot of these issues are close to home if not for us than for people we know: addiction, domestic abuse, and family dynamics—all the glorious messed-up stuff that can happen in a family. (laughs) Through the characters of Josh and Nora, who got married at the end of season three, we are looking at what really happens in a marriage. So it is not just about them as monsters, but it is about exploring what really happens to a couple as they mature together.

Fahy: Yeah . . . I mean what happens if Josh just doesn't want to do the dishes? You probably wouldn't want to push that argument too far.

Fricke: (laughs)

Fahy: Another rich aspect of this show is the music. Many episodes even borrow their titles from songs. Can you talk a little bit about

Josh Levison, a werewolf, and Aidan Waite, a vampire, struggle to live "normal," human lives in *Being Human* (Syfy). "There Goes the Neighborhood: Part 1" (Season 1, Episode 1). © Syfy.

the role of music in *Being Human*? What were you looking for in regard to its musical character and was this type of music integral to your original vision for the show?

Fricke: In season one, Jeremy and I unabashedly wanted to be *Friday Night Lights*; we wanted to be the supernatural *Friday Night Lights*. (laughs) I think Jason Katims is the king of weaving music into his shows, and we love the dimension that can add to a television show. For us, we wanted to have an indie feeling to the score, and in fact we wanted the whole show to feel like an indie film in a way—a little rough around the edges and gritty. So we wanted the music to have that same quality; of course, the truth is we couldn't afford anything else either. (laughs) So we bring in a lot of younger indie artists and a lot of Canadian artists since we film in Canada. This music is also a way to have the show feel young and real. And *Friday Night Lights* was the archetype of having those moments of poetry that music can infuse a show with.

Fahy: Is music an important part of your process as a writer? Do you find that you listen to this music as you are writing? Is it an important source of inspiration?

Fricke: It's funny because it has kind of changed for me. Music is important to me as a person, but I have never really been one of those people who listen to music when I'm writing. It always distracted me, but all of the other writers on the show are always writing with their headphones on. I used to ask them, "How do you guys do that?" But this season when I really needed to buckle down and concentrate, especially on the finale ("Ruh-Roh"), I started listening to music. So at the very end of the season, I finally started listening to music. (laughs) And it really is great. I always thought that it would take away or that I would find myself copying the song somehow, but it does have a great additive quality. I think it is sort of like running with music. I never used to run while listening to music either, but the second you start running with music, you realize, "Wow, this is so much better!"

Fahy: I'm so much less conscious of the pain I'm going through.

Fricke: (laughs). Yes, I can't hear myself breathing heavily anymore. It's so much better.

Fahy: When you look back on that experience writing the last episode of season three, did listening to music while writing change the rhythms of what you were writing? Did it impact your approach to dialogue in any way?

Fricke: I can't listen to just anything, and it depends on what the scene is. Writing season four, I found myself listening to The National a lot, and it was really great writing to it. Their music is so beautiful, but it is also very haunting and often slow. It always feels sort of epic. It's nice; it makes me feel like whatever I'm writing is a *great* scene. (laughs) Of course, if The National is playing in the background, the song is probably a lot better than the scene. But I can't listen to anything too poppy or too happy.

Fahy: When did you know that you wanted to be a writer and how did you find your way to television as an outlet for that?

Fricke: Growing up in Maine with parents who were English teachers, I seemed to always be doing creative writing and theater. Those were the two big things I always did, and I continued that into college. I went to Swarthmore College, and they didn't then (I don't know if they do now) have a formal screenwriting program or television department. You could study those things, but you could only really take creative writing, poetry, and straight-up drama. I kind of was deciding which side to be on, and I think the life of an actor is too difficult, too painful. (laughs) It's easier for me to sit down and have the page in front of me. But I always had done both things—theater and writing—and I moved out to Los Angeles right after college to get a job in television. I sort of learned on the job. I was an assistant for years and worked on it there. I learned from the people around me, and that is how I got my first script. And I just stuck with it from there.

What I really like about TV is collaborating with other people. You write your own scripts. You still have those moments of solitary writing, but for the rest of the time, at least the way we've always done it, you are sitting in a room with people talking about the story and coming up with what the best possible idea can be. You have people to bounce things off of and get feedback from. Then you get to go back into your writer hole. You know that eventually you will be able to come out of that writer hole again and see other people and see it happen on screen.

Fahy: Now that you are in the environment of TV writing, do you find that your sources of inspiration have changed? Are you now more inspired by other television and film? Or do you find literature an important source for inspiration?

Fricke: I'd say more of it comes from novels actually because I do read quite a bit and so does everyone else on the writing staff. The written word just stays with me more than other shows or movies.

Part of it is that I don't want to be ripping off another show. Sometimes it will just be an idea in a book or a character that stays with me. Often nothing ever really comes from it, but a book will spark a discussion. We will start talking about a book, and everyone will read it if they want to. And it sort of gets us talking: "What I liked about the story was this . . ." And the conversation will spin off in its own direction. So again, I find more inspiration from novels in that way.

During the first season of the show, I had just read Audrey Niffenegger's *Her Fearful Symmetry*—she wrote *The Time Traveler's Wife*. It is a great, weird ghost story and romance novel, and that book haunted me all through season one. Between seasons three and four, I read Stephen King's *11/22/63*, and I was obsessed with it. Every now and then, I will get attached to a story like that. I sort of read everything I can get my hands on, and I fall in love with these different literary characters. I just read *The Goldfinch*, which was epic and sprawling and filled with great characters. When certain characters stick with me, I think to myself, "It's a character like that that I'd like to tell a story about." And that sends me off onto the next thing.

Fahy: To bring it back to the issue of genre, what do you think are some of the biggest pitfalls of horror writing?
Fricke: For us on *Being Human*, and perhaps in general for genre shows on television, there is never enough time or money. However you want to do the special effects of the monster or even the seemingly simple enough scare, we can't ever really do it well. It turns out okay, but I always sort of cringe at those moments. It just never looks that great. (laughs) I mean, it's never going to be a big-budget feature. Even in movies that are big, whenever I see the monster, I think: I wish I hadn't seen the monster. In a movie like *Signs* or *War of the Worlds*, when you see the aliens, I always wish I hadn't seen them. I think it's so much better when you don't see anything. I've always been a believer in less is more anyway because I think what

you don't see is scarier. I understand that some portion of the audience wants to see something. It's just never good for me.

I feel bad saying that it is never good because on our show we have a great group of people who work really hard on that visual element. It's just tricky. There is never enough time to really do it. That is the hardest part. We have a group of people in the writers' room who think it would be great to take the whole house and blow it up or to have a horror sequence where the bathroom is upside down and water is streaming everywhere. But we can't really do anything like that. So it is a little tough coming up with things that are going to be exciting without looking. . . . Well, there is a fine line between what we can pull off and what is going to look cheesy. (laughs)

This is a very specialized aspect of television writing. A straight-up writer doesn't have any concept of what something will cost. The writer thinks, "Oh, we'll just do this, or we'll do that fight sequence." Then you'll hear back from production that this thirty-second moment is $150,000. So then you're left thinking, "Okay . . . is there a cheaper way to do it?" (laughs) Basically, it is an art of finding balance. We turn in scripts with a vision of what we would like to do, and then we ask production to take the essence of those scripts and tell us what we can do. A simple writer is not going to know that because you need a whole team of people to help you balance vision with cost, to help you achieve the scare behind the scare you're going for. It is very strange, and it is a whole part of the job that you don't think about. You turn in your script and feel great that you wrote it. But then you spend a couple of weeks reworking it for cost. You either have a scene that is $96,000 over budget or three days over budget or it can't even be shot. That is the hardest part—hacking away at the story and trying to make sure that you don't lose the wrong stuff.

Fahy: What is the best criticism you've ever received as a writer?
Fricke: I might as well say the very first thing that comes to mind.

This was on my first job, and it was sort of infuriating because it came from one of the actors who gave his own thoughts on the process. (laughs) I think he called it the "Anna Fricke Effect." He said that I had a shotgun effect as a writer, that I basically said the same thing a few different ways back to back. So I'd have three or four lines that said the same thing. Basically, that I rambled and repeated myself, and I took that to heart. Especially coming from prose, as a fiction writer and poet in high school and college, dialogue is something that takes years to really get down. You start out in the beginning thinking that you will just write the way people talk, but that doesn't really work because the way people talk and the way you hear it are not going to be the way an actor performs it. Not everyone hears things the same way. Not everyone is going to hear it the way you do or have the same rhythm. That was probably the best early advice that I got, which boiled down to trying to be a little more careful about what I was actually writing. (laughs)

Part IV

"WHO YOU GONNA CALL?"

Haunted Houses and Other Supernatural Terrors

Dr. Peter Venkman (Bill Murray), Dr. Egon Spengler (Harold Ramis), and Dr. Raymond Stantz (Dan Aykroyd) in *Ghost Busters* (1984). Directed by Ivan Reitman. © Columbia Pictures.

American Horror Story, The X-Files, Millennium, and Final Destination

AN INTERVIEW WITH JAMES WONG

Although there was a time when James Wong wanted to be an astronaut, he eventually turned his attention to television and film. As a television writer, Wong did some of his earliest work on the series *21 Jump Street* and *The Commish*, but his role on *The X-Files* helped catapult the show into one of the most successful and popular in television history. Along with his writing and producing partner, Glen Morgan, Wong also became one of the showrunners for the second season of *Millennium*. He co-wrote, directed, and produced such films as *Final Destination* (2000), *The One* (2001), and *Final Destination 3* (2006). He also served as a producer for the remakes of the horror films *Willard* (2003) and *Black Christmas* (2006). In 2011, he became a writer and producer for *American Horror Story*.

Fahy: I'd like to begin with some of your recent work on *American Horror Story.* What exactly is the writing experience like for this show? Do you sit around the room with the other writers at the beginning of the season and ask, "How can we really scare the hell out of people this year"?

Wong: That is pretty much it. We have a writing room with Tim Minear, Jennifer Salt, and Jessica Sharzer. What happens is that in the beginning of the season Ryan Murphy comes in with Brad Falchuk, and they pitch some ideas. Let's talk about last season. Our whole idea is that we change the story every year except that we use some of our cast like Jessica Lange. So last season Ryan had a wonderful idea about setting the show in an asylum. He said he

wanted to deal with race. He wanted a psycho killer named Bloody
Face. And he even wanted a UFO to be in it. (laughs) So Ryan has
these wonderful ideas, and we have to put them together to see
what will work within the structure of the show. But most of the
details are things that we deal with in the entire season to make it
all come to life.

Fahy: What were some of the things that drew you to the show?
Did you know from the start that each season would be a self-
contained story? And what were some of the things you wanted to
explore as a writer on the show?
Wong: That's exactly it. I read the pilot for the first season, which I
really loved. You know, Ryan is not one to make you wait for anything. There is all this stuff in the pilot, and I thought, "Wow, how
can we sustain this?" Then the kicker for me happened at the end of
the interview. I said, "How do we sustain a ghost story, a haunted
house continually?"

Ryan's answer was that we don't. We change it all after one season. To me, that was the most exciting thing. It was like doing a
miniseries or sort of an anthology within the context of thirteen
episodes. And then doing it again in a different way. I immediately
signed on.

Fahy: It seems in so many ways that *American Horror Story* is a
valentine to horror. There are so many allusions to other classic
horror films and works. When you're writing for the show, are you
consciously thinking about certain allusions that you want to make?
Wong: There are certainly tropes that we do deal with—classic horror tropes. Sometimes we think to ourselves that this seems very
familiar and we need to do our own "American Horror" spin on it.
But other times something reminds us of *Rosemary's Baby*, and we
decide to do that. It is not a hard and fast rule that we should shy
away from everything that has been done before, which is impossible. On the other hand, sometimes we feel we should do it because

Jessica Lange as Sister Jude in the second season of *American Horror Story: Asylum* (Fox). © FX Networks.

some classic horror movie did it, or this is how they dealt with it. There wasn't any conscious rule saying: "Let's not do that because of this." But we sort of do things as we feel them.

Fahy: I wanted to broaden the discussion a bit. In many ways, as a writer, director, and producer, you've been scaring people for a long time. How did you get into horror as a genre?

Wong: I don't know. (laughs)

I don't know how that happened. I really don't. I read a lot when I was a kid from F. Paul Wilson to Clive Barker to Edgar Allan Poe to Stephen King. All of those were influences. But it wasn't a thing where I thought this is what I want to do or this is where I'm aiming my career. It sort of happened because of *The X-Files*, which was an anomaly in itself. When we—Glen Morgan and I were partners—worked on *The X-Files*, we had never done anything in the sci-fi or fantasy or horror [genre] in television. We were doing dramatic cop shows. Our first movie was a thriller/horror film in the vein of *In Cold Blood*, so when we first started on *The X-Files*, there were people who actually questioned whether we were qualified to do this. There were people who said, "What makes you think you can do sci-fi?"

As we went along, I felt like it was sort of always there in our background. We had watched *The Night Stalker*, and we were affected by all of these great shows. Those things are always part of you as you grow up, and they came to the forefront when we had a chance to do them on a show that wanted it.

That's how I came into it.

Fahy: Now that you have a lot of experience writing horror, do you still have certain films and shows that you consider favorites or particularly inspirational to you at this point?

Wong: It's hard to say. There are so many things that are great. There are movies—particularly *Carrie* and *The Shining*—that I always look back on and think of as amazing. To me, it's not just horror. *The Twilight Zone* is a perfect TV show. It combines horror with the fantastic. It doesn't have to be horror to be interesting to me. That was the most influential show for me as a writer in television.

Fahy: It is interesting how that model has changed. In some ways, with *The Twilight Zone*, the model of TV then was a series of self-contained episodes. With *American Horror Story*, you are moving somewhat in that direction again—except with a season-long version.

Wong: I don't think we are moving toward self-contained episodes, though. It is always our goal to have answers. *American Horror Story* definitely gives you answers to questions that you have. We don't drag it out too long. It is just the way that Ryan feels. He wants to give you answers only to pose more questions. You don't have the same question throughout the show. Although the idea of serialized shows is not new, they are new for today. They are the coming trend because people have an ability—because of DVRs or because of Netflix—to watch shows in a row. That is more of a novelistic approach to television. That is what's exciting people these days. I know some friends—lots of friends of mine actually—who record shows on DVR and wait and tell everybody not to talk about the show while they're in the room. They want it in a big burst.

Fahy: Once you're working in this genre, there seems to be a lot of interesting challenges. Horror fans crave novelty, but they also want the familiar (we know something bad is going to happen in that dark basement but we want to go down there anyway). How do you keep it fresh as a writer?

Wong: It's really hard. You have to be cognizant of that. You have to be cognizant of the needs the audience wants fulfilled and of the surprises you can spring. Sometimes it is just working hard and going over lots and lots of scenarios to end up in a place where you feel it is fresh. Sometimes it is just inspiration. When we were working on *The X-Files*, our modus operandi—and how I work generally—was to take a fact from the world and build upon it or twist it. Once you have a fact that people feel familiar with, you can upend their expectations because there is a known factor. That's how I approach trying to do something fresh. We're not always successful, but if you're trying to do something fresh, the audience needs some grounding—some familiarity with what you're trying to present—in order to upend their expectations. If it's completely new, then it's a different experience. So that's how I approach it. There is a backbone or spine to start with that allows you to upend expectations.

Fahy: You mentioned inspiration—where you get your ideas and your inspiration. So you seem to be saying that you're not looking for extreme cases in the news for inspiration, but instead you're looking at the mundane, the everyday through the prism of horror. Is that right?

Wong: Yes. That's what I'm thinking. This is not a hard and fast rule. It works or it doesn't work depending on what you want to do in a particular episode or movie. But my rule of thumb is that if people can run into this situation in their everyday lives then it is ripe for me to exploit it in a horrific way. So when people run into it in their everyday lives, they can think back to that moment in a show or movie and have some fun with it because of that association.

That's why I'm not as interested in torture-porn. It's not likely you're going to be trapped in a dungeon in some strange place. It seems kind of crazy to me. I'm not as attracted to that as I am to regular life twisted.

> "MY RULE OF THUMB IS THAT IF PEOPLE CAN RUN INTO THIS SITUATION IN THEIR EVERYDAY LIVES THEN IT IS RIPE FOR ME TO EXPLOIT IT IN A HORRIFIC WAY."
>
> —JAMES WONG

Fahy: That makes me think of two things. The first has to do with your use of Christmas as inspiration. You worked on the remake of *Black Christmas* in 2006, and in the second season of the television show *Millennium* (the season you were the showrunner), there is a Christmas episode in which Frank Black receives a gift from a colleague—two "holiday" DVDs, *Black Christmas* and *Silent Night, Deadly Night*. The characters then have an amusing debate about whether or not the Santa is a serial killer or a spree killer. In the second season of *American Horror Story*, you introduced a Santa serial killer, Leigh Emerson, in the episode "Unholy Night." Some news networks might say you have a war against Christmas.

Wong: (laughs)

Fahy: But seriously, is this an example of what you're talking about? Finding horror in the everyday?

Wong: Absolutely. If you take the most heartwarming and fuzzy-feeling holiday, that is what you got. When you look at the legend of Santa Claus, it's a little crazy. This guy creeps into your house.

Fahy: Yes, it is a very creepy thing—and we're supposed to give him cookies and milk!

Wong: And he judges you! He's watching you all the time. So there is a lot of creepy stuff going on with that legend. You imbue that with this warm, fuzzy Christian, children's holiday, it gets ripe for satire and horror. We went to the well a bunch of times with that. There is definitely something there.

Fahy: You mentioned these torture-horror movies. In some ways *Black Christmas*, like *Texas Chainsaw Massacre* and other early slasher films, are the starting point for these more recent torture-horror films like *Saw* and *Hostel*. You're saying that you don't find them appealing because you don't find the circumstances realistic for most people, so that isn't as exciting or compelling for you. But do you feel these films go too far in some ways?

Wong: I'm just not as interested in how much we can make a person suffer and the grotesque human biology of breaking points—although I do admire movies like *Saw* and *Hostel* for their aggression and for having a point of view. I admire that, but I'm not into it myself. I'm just not as interested in those moments to be exploited for an entire movie. There are absolutely moments in a movie or in a show where such things are legitimate and really terrifying. But if that is the whole theme of the movie, that is when I become less interested.

Fahy: Because those films are particularly gruesome, is there a line you won't cross as a horror writer? Have you ever cut scenes out of your own work that you ultimately thought went too far, were too scary?

Wong: Yeah. And other people have cut it for me. (laughs)

There is some stuff in *American Horror Story* that I wrote and that we shot that I didn't think was gratuitously grotesque; it was just the suggestion that came across as too extreme. Just recently, one shot was cut short that I loved in *American Horror*. I'll give you an example. Dylan McDermott's character is practicing what he feels is the art of his father. He brings a girl in, and she is panicked on this table. He says his line, and the camera moves away from her and follows a trail of blood to this drain that drains into a bucket. To me, that is really terrifying and horrific, but in a way that is not grotesque. It is grotesque in its idea but not in the visual representation of it. To me, that is a really elegant, horrible (in a good way) shot. Ryan thought that was too much, so he cut that short. But I felt there was a kind of poetry to that. So that is an example of something I thought was just brilliantly done by the director, David Semel. I thought it was perfect, but we didn't have the chance to show it to the public.

Fahy: I'm curious about something. Does your own work ever scare you? I realize you're involved in the nuts and bolts of so many aspects of production, but when you finally see it on the screen, does it ever surprise you in a way where you're a little bit scared? Where it works for you as a viewer?

Wong: I don't get scared by it because I know what is coming. I am surprised at the emotions that it can bring out. The suspense always still works. There are times when you jump because you're so surprised by the way the editor and director have put things together. When it's my own movie, there is nothing to surprise me. When I've directed a scene, I know exactly what piece goes in what order. I've built the blocks. When I'm just writing and producing and I see the show, I have some visceral reactions that make me understand that it works.

Fahy: What do you think are some of the biggest pitfalls of horror writing?

Wong: The biggest pitfall would be to set up an expectation that is exactly met, that the viewer can see way ahead of time. Sometimes you mean for the audience to be ahead of you, to enjoy the ride with you, but you don't want them to be ahead of you in a way that takes away the surprise. That is hard to explain exactly. It is sort of a feeling. You fail if the audience is way ahead of you and they are bored by the journey.

Fahy: What was the best criticism you ever received in your creative life?

Wong: The thing that made me understand the art of storytelling a little more happened with the first *Final Destination.* We had test screenings, and the film was going really well. But the ending just left everybody flat. When we were working on it and writing the movie, it felt like the right ending thematically. It made a point. It was this intellectual idea of what death meant and all that kind of crap. (laughs)

In your head, you think this is the idea that works. But the fact is that it doesn't work if the audience is not with you, if they don't want to be there at the time. So when we did the test screenings, I remember trying to hang onto the idea of this thematic ending. But it was just falling flat. And Bob Shaye [former CEO of New Line Cinema] basically said to me, "You've got to come up with something that excites people as much as the beginning of the movie." I don't know what the specific lesson is. It was never put like, "Thou shalt not make the ending more boring than the beginning"— which I guess is the lesson. (laughs) So I wouldn't say it exactly like that, but that is what I got out of it. The ending has got to be better than the beginning. It has got to be as big, or it has to fulfill the expectations. So that was the best lesson.

Fahy: Was there something nagging at you with that film that made you want to come back and do *Final Destination 3* as a writer and director? Was there some aspect of that story that you just had to get back to?

James Wong directing *Final Destination 3* (2006). New Line Cinema/Photofest, © New Line Cinema.

Wong: Well, it was almost the technical challenge of it. It was the roller coaster sequence. I really wanted to do that roller coaster death. (laughs)

New Line guys pitched it. I loved the building blocks of those movies, and I love putting together all the little pieces that make those scenes. So it was sort of a technical challenge. First of all, we couldn't get anybody in the whole United States to let us even use a roller coaster. We went everywhere. It became a task that was harder than it looks on the film. So it was fun that way.

Fahy: Is it difficult for you or was it a natural transition from writer to director?

Wong: To me, it was pretty natural because when I'm writing screenplays I really look at it in my head as how the scene plays. I'm writing as it plays in my head. So I knew how I wanted it to go. So I really thought visually in that regard. It felt like a natural progression for me.

Fahy: Can you talk a little bit about your newest project, the television series *Occult*?

Wong: We're about to shoot in the middle of June. I'm very excited. We have a great team. The premise is sort of *X-Files*-like in the sense of two FBI agents dealing with a kidnapping. One of the FBI agents is really into the occult. She is sort of an outcast because of her belief in the occult in her past. In the course of this investigation, the other FBI agent actually gets possessed. It is not a possession of the Linda Blair-type. He has to struggle with fighting off this entity inside him for the series. So it's a little bit of a twist on the premise. We have Lynn Collins as one of the leads and Josh Lucas as the other lead. The show is for A&E, and I think it will be released next summer.

Haven

AN INTERVIEW WITH JIM DUNN

Jim Dunn came to Hollywood with the intention of writing comedy, but he soon found opportunities to tap into his passion for horror, science fiction, and fantasy with his work on *The Dead Zone* and the series *Haven*, which he co-created with Sam Ernst. He is currently a staff writer on *Crisis*, and he is creating a new series for ABC based on Stephen King's short story "The New York Times at Special Bargain Rates."

Fahy: Why *The Colorado Kid*? What was it about that particular Stephen King story that inspired you to develop it into a series?

Dunn: We were approached to do it. Well, I'll back up a step. Sam Ernst, my writing partner, and I wrote some movies for independent producers back in the day, and we met a man doing development independently for these producers named Adam Fratto, who later got a job as a development executive at Piller/Segan Production Company. He then asked us to come in and pitch TV ideas to him, and we wound up selling a pilot to ABC. About a year or so later, he approached us because they had gotten the rights to *The Colorado Kid*—or they thought they could get the rights, I should say—and he asked us if we could come up with any good ideas for it. We actually pitched an idea that was true to the book, which doesn't have anything explicitly supernatural in it. The book is about two old newspapermen telling tall tales, and it explores the idea of how too many questions make for a bad mystery. So we tried to develop a TV idea out of that, and it got sent to Stephen King, who sent it back and said, "Yeah, but where is the supernatural stuff?" So we came up with this whole idea of a town full of people with Troubles, with curses that popped up once a week or so, very conveniently, and we sent that off to Stephen King and he liked it. He was a fan of the idea, and he liked our writing. That is sort of how the whole project got rolling. We wound up taking very little from the book explicitly, but there were ideas in the book that we always wanted to hold onto. One of the questions that we found really interesting was: How does a community react to something like this? We had this idea that the curses, the Troubles, ran in families, so how does that shape a community? What does it do? What secrets lie hidden?—which is a very Stephen King viewpoint.

Fahy: What made you decide on the name "Haven" as opposed to keeping King's title? Did you feel it was simply too different from the original?

Dunn: I don't think the book—by Stephen King standards—sold that big, and there were aspects of the title that were problematic for a TV series. The story was not set in Colorado, for instance. Titling a TV series is tricky business in any event. Ideally, you capture something about the essence of the show, and if you have an intellectual property that you are working with, you somehow reference it. Nothing about *The Colorado Kid* as a title really worked for that. We initially titled the show *Sanctuary*, actually. I guess it was originally *Haven*; then it was *Sanctuary* for a while, and then it went back to being *Haven*. There was something about that idea of a town that is a haven for people with problems that remained at the heart of it.

Fahy: A few years before *Haven*, you worked on another TV adaptation of King's writing—*The Dead Zone*. How did you get involved with that project and can you talk about some of the ways that King has inspired your own writing?

Dunn: That was the same production company—Piller/Segan. We developed that pilot with them, and they got a sixth season pick up for *The Dead Zone.* There was a little break in-between, and they had worked with us in the meantime so they offered us a job as staff writers on that show.

It's funny. We came to Hollywood to do comedy. We sort of stumbled backward into writing hour drama because we always wanted to put more story than would fit into a half-hour format. Sam and I have always been fascinated by issues of identity. The first TV pilot that we sold to ABC was about a town full of people in witness protection. We conceived of this idea and later found out that it actually happened in Orange County [California] back in the 1980s, which was sort of shocking. We are also curious about that idea of second chances and how peoples' lives take turns on them. When you get into horror writing, it does two things: first, it lets you explore those kinds of turns, which are inherently interesting for television and for storytelling more broadly. That is one of the things that provide drama—when people face a sudden change in their world. But genre writing also gives you a certain freedom. The almost *Deus Ex Machina* of the supernatural in horror allows you to put a spotlight on something that might otherwise be tricky in straight drama. The first generation of *Star Trek* did some bold things with that back in the day with race relations and women's rights and whatever. In the more sophisticated modern television world, horror is still an easy way to throw a stark spotlight on issues that you're interested in talking about.

Fahy: You mention the freedoms of writing in the horror genre, but it seems that one of the big challenges of being a horror writer is balancing the audience's desire for familiar conventions with something new. How do you strike that balance and keep it fresh as a writer?

Dunn: That is a good question. I guess that is where the art form comes in—especially in television. It is very easy to step into a set of paint-by-numbers tropes in TV. They work. We have all seen them a hundred times, and there is always the temptation to just do it one more time because people will understand it. In fact, some-times there are pressures from various people involved in the whole ensemble of production to do things that are simpler and more direct, that people are going to get. So there is always a tug-of-war between the more creative version and the more familiar version. One of the things we've found over time is that the most effective approach is to start off with a very simple story, a simple concept of what you are trying to talk about. Then when you get into the details (the specifics of the scene, and the place, and the people), that is where it gets interesting. So if you're lucky, you can strike a balance naturally. In other words, if you build it simply enough to begin with, you can find ways to talk about what interests you without making it so complicated that people can't follow it.

Look . . . I'm a genre guy. I've been a huge science fiction and fan-tasy and horror guy since I was a kid, and so is Sam, for that matter. I've always been fascinated by the new ideas in these genres—their ability to present something novel and different in an engaging way. But especially in TV, the core drive of what makes good television is emotional engagement. What is emotional in the story? It's always a struggle to find a good emotional story that gets you involved with the characters. For a series, the more time you can spend working with your main characters, the better, because people can actually form an emotional attachment to them over time. In *Haven*, it's Audrey, Nathan, and Duke. People really want to know about what is going on with them. The story of the week is just a reason to show up and see them in some ways.

Fahy: You mentioned that you initially came to Hollywood to do comedy writing, and despite the horrific elements of *Haven*, it's clear that humor plays a central role in the show: the witty banter between characters, the almost adolescent awkwardness and play-fulness in the love triangle with Nathan, Audrey, and Duke. How did you view the role of humor in the show? Was humor crucial to your vision of the show from the outset?

Dunn: Neither Sam nor I have ever really been fans of the super-dark version of horror. It has its place, and there are people who do it really well. For us, we have a hard time with that. We are both people who make jokes a lot, and just as the people in our lives are people who run high and low emotionally, stories for us work that way too. If something is really dark, you want that counterpoint of humor. We've never gone quite as far as Joss Whedon does in *Buffy the Vampire Slayer* with that self-referential humor and cultural critique, but I really enjoy that stuff. Even in combat, there is a lot of gallows humor and black comedy in how humans actually confront terrible circumstances.

Fahy: So did it feel like you were moving into less comfortable territory in the third season of *Haven* when you introduced a rather gruesome serial killer known as the "Bolt-Gun Killer"? In some ways, that killer added a darker edge to the show. What inspired that arc, that decision to incorporate a serial killer into the show?

Dunn: You know, the life cycle of a TV show is an interesting thing. There are various players involved in making a show happen. Quite often, different people have different ideas about what the show is doing and what you are trying to accomplish. But you don't often understand that until the rubber hits the road, and you are making shows. One of the things that happened early on with *Haven* was that Sam and I always saw it as having a strong serialized component. For us, it was the story of Audrey coming to this town, trying to uncover her exact connection to it, finding lost family . . . and all of those sorts of things. But the network in particular wanted a more stand-alone show. They were looking for an adventure-of-the-week sort of thing. So there was a lot of tension there, and we had less of that serialized component than we wanted in the first two seasons. We kept sneaking it in where we could. Then the network starting having a change of heart after looking at the demographics and at how the show was being received. They also had new ownership with Comcast. So after the second season, they took a different view on what they wanted from the show, and they wanted more of that serialized stuff, which was exactly the sort of thing we had wanted to do. We always had this idea of tying the Colorado Kid from the original book into the show, and from the outset we knew what the Colorado Kid's relationship was to Audrey. We had a seven-year arc for the show in our heads before we started shooting, so when the network shifted gears, we saw that as our chance to bring in the Colorado Kid. By the time we started looking for a way to engage the Colorado Kid, Sam and I pitched the idea that the Colorado Kid would be this serial killer who showed up in town. As we worked on it together as a group of writers, we realized that there was more fun to be had if we kept that character distinct and handed the serial killing off to someone else who was part of his story. While it got darker—and I know it got darker than some people liked—I was really happy with the way that season turned out overall because we were able to bring together a lot of long-running threads that we had been weaving in over the first two years—about what was going on with Haven and Audrey. I felt that in the finale of that season we were able to tie a lot of things together that people really wanted to know about and to give people a pretty full picture of how things worked in this world we had been creating.

Fahy: It must have been fun coming up with Troubles, and there are so many interesting ones: Nathan can't feel anything; Jordan's touch renders one unconscious; a woman stuffs her dead son like a taxidermist. Do you have a favorite Trouble?

Dunn: I remain fond of her—you mentioned the woman who stuffs her son like a taxidermist. I wrote that episode and came up with that Trouble all by myself in some feverish moment. In that first season, we only had three writers on staff, and we were all losing our minds trying to keep up with all of the writing that had to get done. There was a version of that story that I liked even better that was very much a Pinocchio tale. It was about a boy who was stuffed, and in order to stay alive, he had to kill his own father (the man who stuffed him) to make the curse transfer. I don't remember how we worked it all out, but we decided that story was a little too dark. (laughs) I felt that the episode as produced had some problems. It was hard for us to pull off all the stuffed animals. It worked all right, but it wasn't quite what I had in my mind when I was writing it. But it was novel, and that is what I liked about it. It was a very unusual curse.

It's funny, Tom. It's hard for me to pick a favorite Trouble of mine. When Sam and I came in to start the first season, we brought in a list of about thirty Troubles. They went up on the wall. Every year we would add to them. We would go around the room with everyone pitching new ideas, and we'd add those to the list. So we always wound up sort of mixing things together from different parts of different Troubles. So I have a tough time remembering what ones I wrote or did not have anything to do with. I think one of the favorite Troubles I did not write was by Lilla Zuckerman and Nora Zuckerman, a sister writing team on the show. They wrote an episode called "Audrey Parker's Day Off." It was very much an homage to *Groundhog Day*, but I thought they did a really good job building that story in the context of our world where Audrey, who is immune to these Troubles, would be able to find her way out of a time loop. I think *Star Trek: Next Generation* did about ten episodes with different kinds of time loops that people had to find their way out of. It is always tricky to figure out a new way to do it, and my hat is off to them for it.

But when it comes to something like a Trouble, it is a grab bag. Certainly, there are any number of concepts, ideas you've seen a hundred times. But really it's the fun of getting a room full of geeks together and trying to find a way to put a twist on it that the audience hasn't seen. I showed my seven-year-old son the first episode of the original *Star Trek* with the salt vampire, which was a creative spin on the vampire myth. And he saw the vampire's face and freaked out, and that was the end of watching that for a while. (laughs) It's that kind of stuff. It's looking for an approach that is not completely expected, taking an idea in a direction that is less familiar or more interesting than the same-old, same-old.

Fahy: Earlier you mentioned being a big genre fan, and we've talked about the impact of Stephen King on your writing. What were some of your earliest influences as a writer in film and TV?

Dunn: I watched a lot of *Star Trek* growing up. In fact, Michael Piller of Piller/Segan, the company we did *Haven* with and did our other pilot with, was the executive producer of *The Next Generation: Deep Space Nine*—that whole second wave of *Star Trek*—and his son, Sean Piller, is an executive producer on *Haven*. So I found it interesting working in their building—they own a lovely little building that we used for our offices—and reminders of *Star Trek* are everywhere. The blueprints of the *Enterprise* and various stages that they built are up on the wall. There is a phaser . . . all of this cool stuff sitting around. The thing about *Star Trek*, which is a touchstone for an entire generation of people creatively, is that it was such an open door. It was like *The X-Files*, too, for that matter. They opened a gateway for different ways to tell stories that could be completely creative and original. In *Star Trek*'s case, it had a more sci-fi edge, and *The X-Files* had a more horror and fantasy edge to it. I always felt a little deprived that I didn't get to see more of *The X-Files*. I had a job where I was working the night it aired for pretty much its entire run, so I only saw a dozen or twenty of them.

As for films I admire, at the risk of making Stephen King unhappy, I happen to love *The Shining*. I know he wasn't happy with Kubrick's adaptation, but I find it really compelling horror to watch. It's funny. Horror is a lot like comedy. It's about surprising juxtapositions. You can see it coming. With comedy, you know there is a punch line coming. You know there is a joke coming, but you're waiting to find out what it is going to be. With horror, it's that sense of dread as you're waiting to find out what's coming around the corner. So from a grand Hollywood, grand cinematographic perspective, I really admire *The Shining*. And from just a good horror

movie construct, both *The Blair Witch Project* and *Paranormal Activity*—though I've only seen the first two—did a tremendous job of
playing on the fundamentals of what scares you, of what is creepy,
of what keeps you on the edge of your seat. I admire both of them
a great deal. Another thing I admire about them—now that I've
done a lot of television production—is the simplicity. It's not gigantic special effects. It's not a thirty-story-tall Stay Puft Marshmallow
Man walking the streets of Manhattan. It's just a lamp swinging in
the background, and you are on the edge of your seat. It's so simple,
and you can do it with a piece of fishing wire and a first AD [assis-
tant director] standing out of frame. Suddenly, you have this piece
of horror that is just tremendous.

When we first started shooting *Haven*, we actually pitched the
idea of shooting the show with a handheld camera. Of course, that
didn't go, and there are lots of reasons why not for production and
TV quality standpoints. But I'm a big fan of *Friday Night Lights*. It
was a tremendous show, and I admired the *cinéma vérité* of those
handheld cameras on Connie Britton and Kyle Chandler. They
basically kept three handhelds running, and they would let those
characters talk over each other. It would only be one or two takes
for the entire scene, but they would get everything they needed. It
was fantastic. Sam and I thought that would be a great thing to do
in a horror show on TV. It wouldn't have to be that way in every
scene, but you capture a real sense of dread in horror with that kind
of motion (like sneaking up on someone) or with that first-person
point of view. It just seemed like it would be so much fun. We never
did integrate that into the show as much as I would have liked to.

Fahy: You mention the effectiveness of this approach for horror.
What do you think are the biggest pitfalls of horror writing?
Dunn: The tendency to fall into tropes. It is very easy to do stuff
that has been done before. One of the problems that is going on
in TV these days is that you have a lot of people making TV who
spend their time watching TV. So you start to have the Xerox

problem where you get a copy of a copy of a copy, and the quality declines with every generation. I find it interesting to see what is happening with shows like *The Walking Dead* or *Game of Thrones*, which are fantasy and maybe horror a little bit. They are bringing in fresh voices or novelistic voices, which is freeing these shows from most of the constraints of standard television formula and letting them do very character-centered stories in those worlds. It's not about the bogeyman of the week. It's about how these people are dealing with the bogeymen they live with. So again, the pitfall is that it is so easy to do cheap and easy knockoffs of the things we know.

"HORROR IS A LOT LIKE COMEDY. IT'S ABOUT SURPRISING JUXTAPOSITIONS. YOU KNOW THERE IS A JOKE COMING, BUT YOU'RE WAITING TO FIND OUT WHAT IT IS GOING TO BE."

—JIM DUNN

Fahy: What is the best criticism you have received as a writer?
Dunne: (laughs) Boy, I'd have to sort through the piles of criticism I've received to answer that. I think the biggest, most useful thing I've been taught is to keep it simple. I'm sort of a closet novelist. I haven't written one, but I'm a big fan of books. In creating TV stories, I want to get complex and layered and to do things with just looks or just a shot. There is a place for that. It's not generally the places I've been writing for. (laughs) It is deceptive, too. When you build things that are really complex, it is easy to fool yourself. You start wandering down a path where you are impressing yourself with how cleverly built something is. But really good stories are often very simple stories. If you can just stick to the simple truths of what you are doing and how that affects people, it is often better than busy plot moves—at least from a writing-honesty standpoint.

Fahy: In closing, I wanted to ask about both your departure from *Haven* and your current projects. Was it difficult to leave *Haven* before completing that seven-year arc you talked about? And can you talk a bit about your newest projects, including the Stephen King-inspired show that you are working on?

Dunn: I think it was time for us to move on from *Haven* for any number of reasons, and it was all right. There certainly had been various frustrations getting the show up and running, but we left the show in good hands. In fact, a lot of the same people are still involved with it. Personally, at a certain level, I was getting a little burned out. I had a lot of story I wanted to tell, but I was starting to run out of Troubles in my head. At some point, you need to bring in some new blood, some new people with different angles on things. We are still involved as consultants—only lightly. We are not doing week-to-week stuff, but when we have things we want to say, we can say them and they get heard and taken into account to some extent. So I'm content with it. I had a good three years, and it was a good time to move on.

Aside from that, we have been working on a show for NBC called *Crisis* with Dermot Mulroney and Gillian Anderson and a whole hoard of other people who are very talented. It is very 24-like—a high action adventure story set in Washington, DC. It's a lot of fun. At the same time, starting about a year-and-a-half ago, we've been working on this other Stephen King project. It is based on one of his short stories called "*The New York Times* at Special Bargain Rates," which appeared in one of Mr. King's collections that came out a few years ago—*Just After Sunset*. It's about a woman whose dead husband calls her the day of his funeral, which freaks her out. He says a couple of things to her on the phone that later come true. We took that as the basis for the series, which is a little bit like *The Dead Zone* with that element of foretelling the future. It's a very romantic story in many respects. This woman and her husband have this deep and profound relationship, but he is dead . . . unless he's not. So how does she get him back if she can? As far as she can figure out, the only way to get him back is to keep trying to act on the information that he is passing to her from wherever he is.

The X-Files and Millennium

AN INTERVIEW WITH FRANK SPOTNITZ

After working as a journalist for several years, Frank Spotnitz attended the American Film Institute, and soon after graduating, he landed his first job on *The X-Files*. Spotnitz had always been interested in horror, finding inspiration in classic horror television such as *The Twilight Zone* and films such as *The Exorcist* and *Rosemary's Baby*. His collaboration with Chris Carter continued on Carter's other shows, *Millennium*, *Harsh Realm*, and *The Lone Gunman*. Spotnitz also revived the classic series *Night Stalker* for ABC in 2005.

Fahy: You have been telling scary stories for a long time—from your work on *The X-Files* and *Millennium* to your remake of the *Night Stalker* series. How did you first get into horror? Were you interested in the genre before joining *The X-Files* or is this something you began to explore more intensely after you started writing for the show?

Spotnitz: I've always been interested in horror and have always tended to write scary stuff. I don't know why exactly, other than scary stuff made a huge impression on me when I was a kid. I was just drawn to it. I connected to it emotionally. In television, *The Twilight Zone* first and foremost and then *Night Stalker*—the two TV movies *Night Stalker* and *Night Strangler* more than the TV series—were hugely influential for me. As for film, *Rosemary's Baby*, *The Omen*, and *The Exorcist* were all giant influences on me. While I was doing *The X-Files*, I thought a lot about what made those films so great. We had to do such a huge variety of stories on the show, and after a while, you want to figure out why some of these stories are working well and why others are such a struggle. Actually, this became one of Chris Carter's maxims during that series: the more believable it seems, the scarier it is. I think *Rosemary's Baby* and *The Exorcist* are models of that. They just seem so plausible. Even if you are a skeptic and an atheist, it is hard not to be *freaked* out. That has always been my strategy in the genre—to really get under the viewer's skin and to make it seem like it could be happening to you. The other thing that those two films did extremely well was that they put you inside the head of those characters. You were so clearly in the point of view of either Mia Farrow or Ellen Burstyn that you couldn't help identifying with them and feeling terrified along with them. I love that. It's so great.

Fahy: You mentioned being a fan of *The Twilight Zone* and *Night Stalker* when you were a kid. Did your interest in those types of shows make you feel like you could write for something like *The X-Files*? Did you think, "I can tell these kinds of stories"?

Spotnitz: Yes, but it was not a seamless transition I have to say. (laughs) My first career was as a reporter, and after doing that for seven years, I went back to film school. *The X-Files* was my first job out of film school. In some ways I got the job at *The X-Files* a little too early. I was so green. My writing skills were pretty uneven when I first got hired, and I think the only reason I hung on is because I did have this intuitive understanding of what a story should be. It took a few years for my craft to catch up to my intuition. Actually, now that you're saying it, something just came back to me that I had forgotten about. When I was five years old, I lived in Aurora, Colorado, and there was a Friday night movie that was hosted by a local gas-station owner. He was kind of an odd guy who would show these horror films. It was very campy stuff, but these movies scared the *crap* out of me! I was only five at the time, and my brothers, who were much older than I was, would take me. But that is probably where it began. That is probably why I went on to watch *The Twilight Zone.*

Fahy: You just mentioned how you developed your writing skills on *The X-Files*, and of course, the series recently celebrated its twentieth anniversary. In hindsight, what were the most valuable lessons that you learned as a writer from *The X-Files*—particularly in terms of the art of storytelling?

Spotnitz: It really was my second film school, and it couldn't have been a better one. This is largely because of Chris Carter, who was an incredibly demanding boss. He really insisted that you do your best, and he wouldn't rest until he felt you had. That is the first thing that I learned from him and from doing that show: ambition. You must be trying to write the greatest thing ever. You're not going to end up doing that, but you have to try or it won't even end up being good at the end of the day. Then you have to be as smart as you can possibly be. That is not something I necessarily appreciated at the time. I had been raised on primarily '60s and '70s TV, where shows like *The Twilight Zone* were the exception. As far as Chris was concerned, you couldn't be smart or sophisticated enough for the audience. The work ethic behind that sort of discipline of not stopping until you didn't know what else to do to make it better was incredibly important to me.

Fahy: Along those lines, I'd like to ask you about two of your standalone horror episodes in *The X-Files*: "Our Town" (about a small Southern town that practices cannibalism as a means of staying young) and "Detour" (about a pair of Mothman-like killers that have learned to camouflage themselves almost perfectly after hundreds of years of surviving in the woods). Can you talk a little bit about some of the things that inspired those episodes?

Spotnitz: "Our Town" was my first stand-alone episode, and I literally sat there in my office thinking, "What is the scariest thing to me?" And being eaten by somebody else is up there on the list. This was very early in the development of the Internet, and it was certainly before I knew how to do research on the Internet. So I went to the UCLA research library, and in all the books I could find on cannibalism, the pages that I was looking for had been torn by students. So I knew I was onto something! Somehow, I stumbled upon this Creutzfeldt-Jacob disease, which was obscure back then. This was well before the mad-cow scares with beef in Europe that came along years later. My brother is a neurologist, so I called him and got a lot of very free and easy research on how that terrifying disease is transmitted. And I think I had a bit of *Deliverance* in there, too. Not literally. But the idea of being in a small town and in a hostile, unfamiliar environment is at the heart of that story too. Those are the two things that inspired me to write that episode.

As for "Detour," the original reason I wanted to do that episode was honestly because the show was hugely expensive, and I was trying to think of an episode we could do where there would be no sets. And one of the questions that always occurred to me when I was in the woods was: What are all those sounds? What are all those things around me that I can't see? That led to the idea of chameleons, and from there came the rest of the story. The irony of it was that it ended up being a very expensive episode because we had *terrible* weather—unseasonably bad weather. So we had to keep reshooting and reshooting, and we even had to build a set. In that scene by the fire where Scully sings that Three Dog Night song ("Joy to the World"), we had to build it on stage because the weather was so terrible. So it didn't work out cost-wise. (laughs)

Fahy: That moment when Scully sings to Mulder gave a glimpse of the depths of their intimacy, but its context was also a reminder of the ways their relationship in general was forged by trauma. I'm curious about your thoughts on the role of trauma and suffering in their relationship.

Spotnitz: I think you're absolutely right, and that is absolutely central to their relationship. It is what makes their relationship interesting. The very thing that brought them together was the very thing that kept them apart—which was their work. Like any good drama, trauma or conflict defines character. You got to see the quality of

Fox Mulder (David Duchovny) and Dana Scully (Gillian Anderson) get back to fighting monsters in the dark in *The X-Files: I Want to Believe* (2008). Directed by Chris Carter. 20th Century Fox/Photofest, © 20th Century Fox.

Mulder and Scully's heroism when they were put through these dreadful situations. It was terribly romantic without necessarily being sexual. They were almost never sexual, but it was terribly romantic to see the sacrifices that these two people would make for each other through the crucibles they were put in.

Fahy: Speaking of characters forged by traumatic experiences, I'd like to ask you about Frank Black. Was it difficult to write for *Millennium* given its particularly dark and bleak tone?
Spotnitz: It's funny because honestly that's where I feel really comfortable, and I think Chris Carter, too. I don't know why, but for the two of us, the darker it was the more we liked it. (laughs) I still think that first episode of *Millennium* is one of the best pieces of writing that Chris has ever done, and that is saying a lot. He has done some amazing writing. It was so dark and so disturbing. But the problem we had with *Millennium* was that the network—probably justifiably—was terrified of its darkness. They kept wanting

us to find ways to leaven it, and it just didn't feel right. We wanted it to be very, very dark. Chris and I ended up having much more to do with the first season than we intended. Honestly, Chris had hoped these other writers would come in and kind of run with it. But that didn't happen. We ended up being full time on two series that year—*The X-Files* and *Millennium*—as well as the first *The X-Files* movie. That was no question the hardest year of my life. Glen Morgan and James Wong came back for the second season, in part, to give Chris and me some relief. But also we wanted to try and find a way to make the show less oppressive for the general public. I'm not sure they did. They took it in a really interesting direction, but the subject matter remained dark—and it was that element that appealed to people. Even though the show only lasted for three seasons, I still hear about it almost as often as I hear about *The X-Files*. There are still a lot of really devoted fans of that show because it had an intensity and purity to it that people still respond to.

Fahy: In some ways, it is very much a show about family. One of your early episodes, "Weeds," is about a small community in which a serial killer is targeting the sons of fathers who have committed sins but never come clean about them. Family life was also integral to Frank Black's character. What do you feel the show was saying about family? And do you think Frank Black was a good father?

Spotnitz: I do think he was a good father and a good man. He was a genuine hero. To me, you are hitting on what made the darkness bearable for me as a writer and for audiences. You can't just have these serial killers, these people who are the embodiments of evil on earth. You need that yellow house. In the first two seasons, it was important that Frank needed to protect Catherine and Jordan. You need the light and the innocence that you are trying to preserve to fight off the darkness. There is a beautiful scene in the first episode when Catherine confronts Frank about that. She tells him that you can't block out the outside world, but Frank says, "I want you to make believe that I can."

The other aspect about this that I've thought about a lot in the years since *Millennium* is that I do think the world is full of all this darkness and evil. And it is a terrifying place if you really open your eyes to it. But I also think that light and love are actually more powerful. There are plenty of terrible, terrible things still happening in the world, but if you look at the course of human history, things get better in the long haul.

Fahy: Is there an episode of *Millennium* that you wrote that you feel best typifies what the series was trying to do?

Spotnitz: The favorite episode that I wrote was "Sacrament" in season one, which is the one that most clearly suggested that Jordan had inherited something of what Frank had. The episode had the idea of the horrors hidden within houses you drive past. From the outside, you would never guess the terrible things going on behind those walls. Frank's brother's wife is literally entombed behind a wall in the home of the man who has taken her, which I find terrifying. Overall, the best episodes for me were the pilot and another episode that Chris did in season one called "Lamentation," which introduced Sarah Jane Redmond's character Lucy Butler.

In the third season, one of my favorite episodes that year was "Antipas," which was also a Lucy Butler episode. It deliberately echoed *The Innocents* with Deborah Kerr, the great film adaptation of Henry James's story "The Turn of the Screw."

Fahy: You just described this period on *Millennium*, *The X-Files*, and the first *X-Files* movies as the most difficult year of your life. I would imagine that one of the challenges involved the diversity of demands as a writer—shifting from horrific to humorous episodes, as was often the case on *The X-Files*; capturing Frank's insights into the minds of serial killers; and creating the broader mythology for *The X-Files*. So as a writer, you had to wear a lot of hats, so to speak. Were those demands difficult to navigate? Did you prefer one style in particular?

Spotnitz: Yes, it was incredibly difficult. In fact, all eight years of *The X-Files* were incredibly difficult. It was a very demanding job, and we never stopped trying our best. But I would say in one sense *The X-Files* was easier because *The X-Files* embraced the supernatural wholeheartedly. To me, when you depart from literal reality, it is an invitation to have something to say. You must have something to say, or it is not going to be an interesting story. All monsters are exaggerations of human beings. You are making that exaggeration to make a point—not so much to lecture at the audience but to ask a question or to shine a light on something. That was really my guide many, many times in *The X-Files*. I intuitively came up with an idea for a monster or a visual, but I could develop it because I realized that it tied into some bigger idea that was interesting.

Conversely, *Millennium*, especially in the first season because we kept a pretty tight rein on the supernatural element (it grew but it was minimal), adhered more to reality, and that was much harder. To me, madness as a motive for a killer is not interesting. We had to find serial killers who had interesting arguments—arguments that had a point. That was the genesis of "Weeds." I wanted to explore the hypocrisy of the people in this small, gated community, and I thought that message would be interesting to explore through the mind of a twisted, sadistic killer. (laughs) But as a writer, I found that to be a more difficult process than just dealing with the frankly supernatural.

Fahy: Is your interest in the supernatural what inspired you to play such a significant role in the mythology episodes of *The X-Files*?
Spotnitz: It was a complete accident. The first time I had lunch with Chris and Howard Gordon, who was Chris's second-in-command at that point, I asked them a question: "It has been a long time since Mulder's sister was abducted. What if some young girl showed up and looked kind of like his sister and said, 'I'm your sister'? What would he do?" I could see the look on Chris's face—*That is a great idea!* That became my first episode. From then on, he kept

looking to me whenever it was time to do a mythology episode. You know we use the word "mythology" now, but at the time, we didn't use that word at all. We didn't really understand the format the series was going to follow. It sort of evolved over the next two seasons. I just ended up being in a role I never anticipated.

> "ALL MONSTERS ARE EXAGGERATIONS OF HUMAN BEINGS. YOU ARE MAKING THAT EXAGGERATION TO MAKE A POINT—NOT SO MUCH TO LECTURE AT THE AUDIENCE BUT TO ASK A QUESTION OR TO SHINE A LIGHT ON SOMETHING."
>
> —FRANK SPOTNITZ

Fahy: I guess you never know what is going to happen when you have lunch with Chris Carter.

Spotnitz: Yeah, you have to be careful. (laughs) It worked out, though. I was happy.

Fahy: I'm curious if you still consider yourself a fan of horror. I ask in part because Chris Carter has recently said that after *The X-Files* and *Millennium* that he was ready to leave behind the darkness of those shows and move in a different direction as a writer. Do you feel that way or are you still drawn to horror works?

Spotnitz: I'm still very much drawn to it. I'm not necessarily drawn to that particular subject matter as a writer only because I've spent so much time thinking about it and mining stories that I don't know what new things I'd have to say for *The X-Files*. I'd certainly like to finish that story, but I don't want to do another five years of *X-Files* episodes. I still find genre storytelling and supernatural storytelling—the kinds of stuff that the late Richard Matheson pioneered—to be my favorite. Well, that's not exactly true. I think the spy genre might be my favorite, but supernatural horror would be a close second if not neck-in-neck because of what I said before. You so often have the satisfaction of knowing why you are writing what you're writing. You have the opportunity to create a really engaging story, and I think this genre is what cinema does best. The power of suspense on film is hard to match in any other medium. Knowing that you have something to think about after the story is over and the entertainment is done. I really like that aspect of it.

Fahy: What do you think some of the biggest pitfalls are in horror writing?

Spotnitz: There are a lot of horror movies that are not about anything, or what they are about is not terribly interesting. They are exercises in brutality and sadism. I'm not saying that to judge; I just don't find that particularly entertaining or interesting. I don't object if other people do. To me, I can tell when I'm watching a science fiction movie or a horror movie and the author has something bigger in mind. I just love that. That really gets me excited when I see a movie or watch a show that fulfills the promise of the genre. I'm afraid that's not what happens most of the time.

I remember when I was in college there used to be a film festival in Los Angeles that held a seventy-two-hour film marathon. So you would arrive Friday, and you would stay until Sunday night—having seen seventy-two hours of movies in a row. I did it once, and the year I did it the festival focused on horror movies. I stayed in that theater for *three* days watching horror movies! After a day and a half, the storytelling becomes so familiar to you because you've been bombarded with horror stories to the point of having sensory deprivation. But the films were quite good. I think the problem for me—apart from the lower-budget horror films—is that big-budget, Hollywood horror or supernatural films start out with really interesting ideas and then they throw them out about halfway through the movie. There are any number of big Hollywood blockbusters—big, successful movies that make gazillions of dollars—that start out with really interesting science fiction notions about terrorism or good and evil or what the quality of heroism is, and then about halfway through the movie because they need things to explode, all of those interesting ideas that they talked about at the beginning are essentially abandoned in favor of spectacle.

Fahy: What is the best criticism you've ever received as a writer?

Spotnitz: I'm sad to say that I've never gotten a review—even a good review—that helped me, that gave me better insight into what I was doing. I am one of those people who do go online, and I read all the fan comments. Of course, you can read a thousand nice things, but it is the one nasty comment that you will never forget. But I remember in season three of *The X-Files*, I had been at a fan convention in Minneapolis, and somebody said that we had completely dropped the ball on the death of Scully's sister: "She lost her sister, and you haven't even talked about it. What kind of crap is that?" And I thought that this person was absolutely right. So on the plane back from Minneapolis, on that one flight, I essentially wrote the story for "Piper Maru," which picked up on the death of Scully's sister, which had been a huge oversight on our part. That was very helpful.

But the best criticism I've gotten has been from my fellow writers on the shows I've done because they are so finely attuned to what I am trying to do and they are really constructive in trying to help me achieve it. That is one of the glories of television and one of the reasons American television is so good right now—because of its collaborative system.

INDEX

CPSIA information can be obtained at www.ICGtesting.com
Printed in the USA
BVOW05*0257300115

385444BV00002B/5/P

9 781628 462012